rethink
PERFECT
The Upside of Uncertainty
–and the art of moderating
our own disputes.

By
Desmond Sherlock

Published by
amibro.com

Rethink Perfect – The Upside of Uncertainty

Designed by Amibro

Published by Amibro, Brisbane
ISBN: 978-0-646-57308-3

Contents

Acknowledgements

I would like to thank Steve, my brother and friend, who believed in my more primitive concepts from the beginning when I explained that "I could be wrong". Without Steve's feedback and support, I think I would have given up a long time ago.

Thanks to my editor, Kristina, who lifted my words up and possibly made a silk purse out of a sow's ear.

Thanks to Kate for our experimental relationship. Our disputes were an essential contribution to developing Rethink Perfect.

Finally, my biggest thanks go to my mum for allowing our dispute, only recently resolved, to play out over the course of 24 years. It was through this dispute and her patience that helped me form many of the concepts that make up "Rethink Perfect".

Des Sherlock

"No matter how thin you slice it, there will always be two sides." Baruch Spinoza

Dedication

This book is dedicated generally to anyone that has an ongoing dispute, and specifically to anyone that has a dispute with me.

First, let me say that I am sorry! With the knowledge I now have, I realize that I should not have entered into conversation until we had agreed to some rules of engagement. The fact that we conversed and are now in a dispute, without an agreed upon method to resolve it, speaks volumes.

Please accept my apology and allow me to suggest that, from now on, we use the principles described in *Rethink Perfect; The Upside of Uncertainty,* to get an agreement, in principle, before any future conversations occur.

"Let our advance worrying become advance thinking and planning".
Winston Churchill

Introduction

Caution, this book comes with a warning. It is not perfect and has yet to be scientifically tested. This theory has only one sample of a Rethink Perfect Agreement, which is presently in use between my brother and me. And that is being sorely tested on a continual basis. I recommend that you do not try to retrofit any disputes that you already have. Better to simply apologise for not having explicit rules of engagement in place before the dispute, and apply Rethink Perfect from now on. This is not a *science* and hopefully not a religion but *the art of moderating our own disputes* and a work in progress.

A Test of a First Rate Intelligence: F. Scott Fitzgerald famously said that, "The test of a first rate intelligence is the ability to hold two opposed ideas in the mind at the same time, and still retain the ability to function." Rethink Perfect is a "test of a first-rate intelligence". I like to think it is a combination of "glass half full" AND "glass half empty" thinking. Or perhaps it is the art of being pragmatic AND a dreamer, the ability to hold both opposing and contradictory outlooks at the same time. What is really new, I think, is my application of Rethink Perfect on interpersonal relationship theory, and the tools that I have spun off that act to moderate us and our disputes.

Think of a thought, an idea, a concept, a feeling, a product that you feel certain is just right, fully developed or perfect. Now ask yourself, are you willing to rethink it? If you have found an idea that you are not willing to rethink, then learning to be open to

1

the notion is the essence of Rethink Perfect. Maybe you are certain that you do not consider any idea to be perfect. Then I would ask you to remember the last time you thought that you were in the right and someone else was in the wrong. Are you willing to rethink your position now? If so, great and welcome to Rethink Perfect thinking. This practice is designed to reduce or control the bias of certainty in our thinking that drives much of our decision-making process, and which also is the underlying cause of our disputes, in my view.

Rethink Perfect is designed to reduce the emotional and intellectual stress (post conversation dissonance) of engaging with people that express dissent. It consists of six proposed rules of engagement, to be agreed to, before we converse. Why is diversity important in relationships? Because it is diversity and its dissenting views that offer us more alternatives to choose from, when innovating or trying to make new and successful decisions. It is "coordinated behavior" or conformity that can cause extreme events, such as the subprime market crash in 2008, or the dot-com crash in 2000, or mass suicides like those of Jonestown, plane crashes through pilot error or even young people marrying too early because all of their friends are doing the same thing. Presently, I believe our society is experiencing a prolonged episode of coordinated behavior. The ongoing statistics of personal disputes, divorce and breakups point to a continual crash culture rather than a single crash event. Rethink Perfect is my attempt to responsibly introduce diversity and dissent back into the subject of relationship and matrimonial disputes, so that we can come up with new solutions to interpersonal problems that exist in the world today.

Rethink Agreements: As far as I am concerned, no agreement is perfect or can be relied upon for certainty. Agreements are only as good as the understanding of the available information used to create them. This understanding can change on a day-to-day or even minute-to-minute basis. Understanding and agreeing to the limitations and ultimately the uncertainty of agreements is part of the first principle of

Rethink Perfect. It is the first agreement of what I call "Rethink Agreements". As we continue to relate, it is likely that this information and our understanding will change continually and we will desire to revisit this, our first agreement, and any others we have formed. Understanding this, I think you will see that it will be necessary to have a robust method or framework of engagement, however new and untested, that we can use to deal efficiently with future conversations in order to disprove, resolve and improve on any previous Rethink Agreements.

This type of thinking is not for everyone, as it requires a shift from how we normally think and talk, as it exposes our illusion of control or certainty. However, if we did agree to use Rethink Perfect, could we have a war or even a fight? Somehow I doubt it. Heck, we could not even fight for the idea of Rethink Perfect, since, even it is worth rethinking. Rethink Perfect is an agreement of uncertainty or an agreement we have while not having an agreement.

The First Principle: Whatever we think, hear, say or see could be wrong, or is at least flawed. From this basic idea follows everything in this thesis. If you reject outright the principle that anything and everything is open to rethinking, then it is quite possible that this book is not for you. That is not to say that you are "wrong". Within the framework of my dissertation, I have to assume that I have not yet refined my ability to convincingly explain this first premise. Or perhaps your concern is that agreeing to this principle would imply a commitment to follow through or follow some leader. Or it may be that at this point, you cannot envision retrofitting your life and other relationships with new kinds of thinking. That is understandable but not exactly necessary, in my view, but change would be inevitable. However, if you have any unreasonable fears at this point, I would suggest you do yourself a favor and stop reading, as I do not think that you will get much more out of this book. If you do continue and subsequently find yourself scoffing at some of the ideas, don't say I did not warn you. If you wish to make any complaints after this point, please try to do it responsibly. See more about this in chapter 3.

Why I Wrote This: The concept of Rethink Perfect has been crystallizing over the course of the last 26 years. First and foremost, this was done for my own benefit, to help me develop as a person by removing any residual dogma or unreasonable certainty and the attendant reactions that they caused in me. It has also been written for and with the help of my brother Steve, who has allowed me to test these concepts and rethink agreements on him through the years. Steve believed in the value of these concepts, even when they were in their more rudimentary form.

My relationship with my mum has also contributed to writing this book. With her, I encountered "irresolvable" issues that at first seemed impossible to overcome. Trying to reach a resolution with my mum over the last 24 years has helped develop Rethink Perfect. Consequently, our relationship is improving.

This book has been designed so that the reader may offer feedback on these concepts. I would like to convert them (my concepts, not the reader's) so that these ideas are more easily understood and can be more easily accepted by the reader and me.

I set out on my quest to see if I could come up with a way to stop demands being put on me, but without me putting my demands back on them. Starting with the biggest and what I consider the most outrageous demand of all, which is to promise that I will remain "committed" to a person for a lifetime. How can I be committed to the "person" when I am continually learning how I prefer to be treated, and as a "person" we are in a constant state of flux and development? How can I also make a "promise" about what I will be thinking or doing tomorrow, let alone for the rest of my life? I cannot allow society to push me into making, what I consider outlandish and ultimately dishonest promises and *com*promises. I believe that such rigorous expectations and demands contribute to the appalling statistics regarding failed relationships and general disputes across the world today.

That is not to say that I advocate dumping the binding legalities involved in such partnerships. I am simply attempting to separate the state from "love". If two people embark on a legal and binding agreement, they should treat it as such and abide by the legal and financial requirements. It is these promises of certainty that I am expected to make in the name of "commitment", "agreements" and "love" that this book will be looking at.

Q. What is the biggest cause of divorce today?
A. Marriage!

That joke is not so very far off the mark. With the advent of Rethink Agreements, no more can someone scream, "But you promised!!" when the other wants to revisit the agreement. Or "You should know better!" implying an agreement already existed, when no agreement was discussed. This does not mean that this concept condones the breaking of agreements. It is incumbent upon Rethink Perfect thinkers to agree to a new Rethink Agreement before the old agreement is made redundant. Thus we get a ratcheting effect from this process of building upon previous agreements.

Q. What is the biggest cause of marriage today?
A. Divorce!

As this joke implies, I think that it is because people can so easily get out of their marriage contract that couples readily make false promises, or so-called commitment. This book is still about commitment, but rather than one person committing to another, it is about being committed to an idea or concept that both can agree to and review at any time. That is Rethink Perfect Agreements.

This book is the result of half a lifetime spent pondering agreements and personal relationships, filling some 50 A5 journals with thoughts, questions, frustrations and eureka moments. Rethink Perfect has been a journey of discovery for me, my mountain to climb. Every day reinforces my decision to undertake the investigation of so many implied agreements, resultant expectations, and the aggression and unhappiness they can induce when we fail to live up to them.

My Epiphany Moment: The title, Rethink Perfect, was derived from an epiphany moment I had in 1985. At the time, I was using my certitude to fight a Christian organisation's dogma, and not getting very far. It finally dawned on me that "I could be wrong" in my thoughts and deeds, which allowed me to abandon my crusade without feeling like a quitter. I applied the "I *could* be wrong" test to other people, to determine whether they could be wrong, too. To my surprise, I found that most people had thoughts that they believed couldn't possibly be "wrong". This discovery led me to look at dichotomies, and how we tend to think in black-and-white or right-and-wrong, with very little room for shades of grey or nuance. Edward de Bono's book from 1990, *I Am Right, You Are Wrong*, with his concepts of parallel talking and thinking, had a big impact on my journey. Influential, too, was *Zen and the Art of Motorcycle Maintenance* by Robert Pirsig, whose protagonist searches for the definition of "quality" and through the process, goes crazy. While reading his book, I coined a new word to describe the opposite of quality: "unquality". I found that it was so much easier to understand concepts like dishonesty, imperfection or uncertainty by looking at them through the lens of unquality or their flawed side. And it possibly saved me a stint in a psych ward.

The Razor's Edge by Somerset Maugham also played a part in my realising that life is for learning, without necessarily going to university. *Black Swan* by Nissam Nicholas Taleb helped me see that the "I could be wrong" theory had been around awhile in the form of Critical Rationalism, which was advanced by Karl Popper, one of the greatest social and political philosophers of the 20th century. "I could be wrong" then evolved in 2010 into "Rethink Perfect". A quick search on the web proved that I was the first person to have coined this phrase. Hopefully, I will not be the last person to try to practice it.

Chapter 1 Perfect Thinking

When I tell people about *Rethink Perfect*, the first reaction seems to be that: "Nobody's perfect", and "You can't work out relationships! They're too complicated!" followed by "It's too time consuming to prepare for all the possible events that can occur" and a final declaration that "We are all different and no one plan can fit all."

Needless to say, I do not agree with their certain limited views. I consider that the saying "He who fails to plan is planning to fail" applies to relationships as much as anything else that we do. As complex as people and relationships are, humans are also blessed with an incredibly complex computing system: the mind. I believe this powerful internal computer can assist us in understanding ourselves, given some time, effort and real conversation. The irony is that while many people spend vast quantities of time and effort planning their wedding day (or pay a fortune for someone else to plan it for them), they seem to balk at the thought of expending as much time and effort to consider improvements in their relationships. It is as though increased awareness might detract from their relationship, rather than enhance them. On the one hand, they seem to be looking for certainty, stability, security and commitment from their relationship, but on the other hand, they seem to desire spontaneity and believe they can't get that with forethought and planning. I think it is still possible to have both and that planning for such awareness can open up a relationship to so much more than we ever thought possible, and maybe even more.

The first thing you might notice is that the naysayers' statements above are designed to goad me into renouncing "this folly", and to conform instead to "accepted thinking". Even though they may concede that they have not got the answers, they seem certain that I don't have any either, and seem determined to make sure that I am not encouraged to continue my quest, deeming it a waste of their time and mine. I would say that that has been the general response from the vast majority of the people I have spoken with about planning for better relationships over the last 26 years. But instead of discouraging me, it was more like a red rag to a bull. The way that they seemed to "protest too much" convinced me that I might be onto something. That something, I now see, is an approach that encourages diversity of thought in two or more people; an approach that supports the free expression of these thoughts, rather than trying to quash new ideas, just because we did not come up with or understand them. Learning to appreciate feedback, regardless of how it is delivered, and attempting to modify my conversation so that others might someday be able to agree with it, seems to form the core concept of Rethink Perfect.

Nobody's Perfect: As the saying goes most people would not argue with its premise. Although, it doesn't really make sense to me, in that it could be more specific. That is, nobody's actions are perfect. But then add time to the equation and we get "nobody's perfect all of the time". Does that mean that somebody is perfect some of the time? Hmmm....? Not such a perfect statement after all and I guess it just proves the point.

So, if I suffer from a constant state of imperfection (which I believe I do), then why is it that we do not have some rules of engagement to deal and cope with these imperfections that are destined to occur and effect others? How are we supposed to act when someone does or says the "wrong" thing? Rethink Perfect has been written to embrace our foibles and allow us to form even stronger connections based upon our imperfections and uncertainties.

So, what is perfection, and does it exist? Can we have a "perfect" relationship, and is it worth planning for? Can perfection have failures? I guess these and many other such questions have been asked since the dawn of time. I will be attempting to answer these questions throughout this book, and I even have a few neat diagrams that help to clarify it. I do believe that "perfection" is a lot closer to us than we imagine, but is not what we may think it to be. For now, let's look at two parts of a person that we all seem to have in common, and see if we can get a Rethink Agreement on these two points.

Our Ears: How many people do you know that enjoy being shouted at, or demanded of, in a tone that is laced with expectations? None that I know of.

Our Mouths: How many people do you know that could profess never to have complained about others behind their backs, or to have never assumed an angry tone in an attempt to coerce someone into acquiescing to their demands? None that I know of, either.

As you can see, these two human parts – ears and mouth - are not compatible and when combined, are likely to put stress on the workings of the relationship. This is not rocket salad and you don't have to be Sherlock to realise that demands, and the aggression associated with them, are not conducive to happy relationships. Demands may produce short-term results, but the attendant stress can exact a high price, such as unhappiness, resentment, breakups – even ill health.

It is self-evident that aggressive demands are likely to happen because of our mouths, but are unacceptable because of our ears. Rethink Perfect has a series of rules, tools and agreements that anticipate the failure of these mismatched human parts. The proposed solutions have been put together by the investigation of what I call our Black Box recorder or experiences. We all have had them, and when investigated or "data mined" through objective observations, these internal recorders can reveal a mountain of information, which is useful for exposing the common causes of failures that occur in relationships, and allows for the creation of common solutions.

Independent Observations: To make this data mining we need to have the experiences (data) and to have taken the plunge into deep conversation and to have the disputes. I guess I am claiming that I can make such "objective" observations having consciously sought such experiences over the last 26 years. My independence comes from never receiving a cent for anything I have written about relationships to date. I am not a member of any psychology or relationship organisation. I am not married. I have no boss. I am not an academic, and I am not an expert. I am not "dependant" on anyone for sex, money, power, support, or endorsement to boost my ego at present.

I suppose that people who are in the trenches of a relationship, or who are affiliated with various organisations, might consider my ideas to be uncertain, underdeveloped and untested. I agree! That should encourage such readers to examine each concept so that they may spot errors in my logic, and simply disprove my reasoning by offering me feedback. However, I feel that observers who are dependant on others might be less than objective and could have their vision clouded by fear. If they asked themselves "Would I be willing to test Rethink Perfect on any of my existing relationships at the risk of losing them?" A tough ask and as you can see, this could explain why relationship theory has changed very little over the last 100 years, as compared to the other sciences.

Our Desire to be Always Right: In one of his latest books, *Think Before It Is Too Late,* Edward De Bono claims that if we can understand the brain's mechanisms, then we can create the thinking "software" to cope with these processes. He also talks about self-organising systems and how our brain is one.

Self-organising systems are those that take the path of least resistance, such as erosion from water, for example, think of water flowing down a mountain.

Diagram 1.

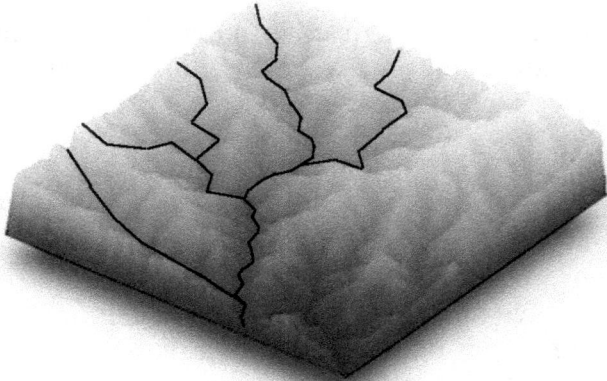

Self organising system.

Rethink Perfect is about understanding the brain's mechanisms to find the path of least resistance. Being "right" or a combination of certitude and the "desire to be always right" forms our path of least resistance in our thinking, but also forms a major problem. I think our desire always to be right is so strong that we seem to insist in making what is not necessarily right into "right", so that we can claim that we have found the path of least resistance, to ourselves and to others. It's a bit like fashioning a "god" or "truth" from a golden calf, because we don't have the patience to wait for the "answer" to come. Or the reverse can also be explained with the term "cognitive dissonance" or by the more commonly used expression, "sour grapes". That is, if we fail to achieve our goal, we pretend it is not what we wanted in the first place, and falsely accuse the desired grapes of being sour.

If we don't have the patience required to find what is actually "right", or the honesty to say that it is only our opinion and potentially flawed, then we will continue to tell falsehoods to others and, more importantly, to ourselves. Worst of all, we actually believe these falsehoods. This explains why we say that we are our own worst enemy, because of this inbuilt bias towards our own certainty, and the desire to always be right.

So what thinking software am I proposing to counter this problem? Well, I think that it already exists and is called "real conversation" or conversing. It is through real conversing that we can find out, from other people's feedback, that what we thought was right was actually not. And this is where some rules of engagement, once agreed to, can assist us with our desire to always be right and the certainty that we actually are. By tapping into the same bias in others, we can naturally get them to act as the "devil's advocate" to help us out of our own bias, just as we can help them out of theirs. As long as we both understand this principle, diverse thinking and expression will be encouraged from both of us.

Seeking Dissent and Diversity: On page 34 of *Think Twice*, Michael Mauboussin's book on harnessing the power of counter intuition, he talks about seeking out dissent by finding data or experiences from "....reliable sources that offer conclusions different than yours. This helps avoid a foolish inconsistency", and "When possible, surround yourself with people that have dissenting views. This is emotionally and intellectually very difficult but is highly effective in exposing alternatives." Rethink Perfect is designed to reduce the emotional and intellectual difficulty of interacting with people with dissenting views.

In Guy Kawasaki's book *Enchantment*, he talks about having a diverse team. "A diverse team helps make enchantment last, because people with different backgrounds, perspectives, and skills keep a cause fresh and relevant. By contrast when a naked emperor runs a kingdom of sycophants and clones, the cause moves towards mediocrity." Rethink Perfect is my way of encouraging and maintaining diverse views during interpersonal relations.

Who Wants to be Wrong: Is there any question that we all desire to be always right, all the time? Okay. When was the last time that you wanted to be wrong? Or when was the last time that you admitted that you were wrong, and how easily does it flow off your tongue? Or when was the last time you said that you were sorry first, and then admitted that you were wrong or had made an error in judgment? I am sure you can do it, but not as often as the errors that you created in your previously flawed judgments. (I'll bet that this is even hard to read now.) I can understand, as I still have trouble putting up my hand.

Why is it that we get angry or agitated so easily when someone does wrong by us? Even if the error was not done intentionally, we can still take it personally when things don't go right (think of road rage). When was the last time you said to someone something like, "Good point, that beats my argument hands down"? Or when things don't go our way we "lose it" and don't even think twice about our anger and where it came from. Rethink Perfect is not only about thinking twice when we lose our cool, but also entails a willingness to evaluate and re-evaluate our thinking processes, in an attempt to avoid those actions that cause grief, both to ourselves and to the people around us.

Balancing the "Desire to be Always Right" is about realising first and foremost that when one of us loses it (our cool), *we* both have lost it (the plot). That getting angry and being right do not go together. It seems that our desire to be always right is so strong that we create all sorts of excuses and/or perpetrators to blame when things do not go right for us. More on this in on page 31.

Still doubt that you desire to always be right? So, when was the last time you told someone to "get over it" or "let it go", or simply refused to enter into a discussion with someone who had an issue with you? Did it ever cross your mind that this might be your way of protecting your desire to always be right? Rethink Perfect is about always being ready and open to engage in a discussion with anyone that has a problem with our behavior. The rules of engagement allow us to have the diverse conversations needed to resolve the effects that our errors have on our own and other people's lives. It is a bit like the Black Box Recorder in a plane. In this case after a *clash* we can examine the contents and see where we went wrong and right during the process. I believe that it is the desire of the airline industry to investigate each and every crash that has made it the safest mode of travel in the world today.

Our desire to be always right leads us to avoid making decisions or to do something different that could result in our being wrong or uncertain. This could explain how a lack of creativity can occur in people. At the same time, to maintain our facade, we put on a front of all-knowing. After all, how can we be certain if we don't know everything? Bluffing and crafting answers from hearsay or loose interpretations, we appear to be wise. For example: how often have you used the phrase "I'm not sure" when you did not have a clue what the actual answer was? Surely it would have been more accurate to simply say, "I don't know".

A funny yet interesting experiment was carried out by Professor John Trinkaus, who is known for dedicating his academic life to the scientific observation of ordinary people going about their everyday lives. In his study "The Demise of Yes", he plotted the verbal trends in providing an affirmative response to an inquiry. Of the 419 questions analysed, 'yes' was only used 53 times, whereas 'exactly' was the affirmation used 117 times, and 'absolutely' appeared 249 times.

The Desire to be Always Right is a Noble Desire!
The desire to be always right is not inherently a bad thing, it just has a few cracks in it. And as Leonard Cohen says, "...that's how the light gets in." After all, it is only a desire isn't it?

Unchecked by colleagues, friends and family, the cracks can grow but as far as a desire goes, I think it is probably the key to human survival (and prosperity) up to now and probably for a while to go.

When he was 12, my nephew said to me in a family counseling session, "You can't always think that you're always right, all the time", like it was a bad thing and I should stop doing it. My more primitive defensive response at the time was "ditto", but after a few months of rethinking, I came up with a responsible reply. Imagine traveling down a highway full of indecisive drivers. If they did not think that their decisions were right, they probably wouldn't get very far. No, I am grateful for this very precious desire that has kept me alive and well for this long. Thinking that I am always right, all the time, (at the time), to me is not the problem; however, "knowing" that I am always right is indeed problematic.

Just imagine that we always thought that we were always right, all the time, at the time (nanosecond) of decision making; that we needed to believe that we were perfectly right or certain in order to make instantaneous decisions; that we lived in a virtual paradox, where we knew that we could be wrong about the next thing we thought about and the last decision we had made. But for the briefest of instantaneous moments, representing "now" or the present, we thought that we were perfectly right. If this were so, then that would mean for any given day, we could average some 20 perfectly right decisions a minute or some 20,000 of them daily. I believe that this is how our mind actually works. Imagine the effects such thinking could have on our general thinking and planning. Heck, it might even explain how people can claim that they can guarantee to stay with someone for a lifetime, almost as though they could make an instantaneous thought last a lifetime. However, we all know the statistics: as many as 1 out of 2 reading this have already experienced the effects of having such unrealistic promises made to them, or perhaps have found themselves on the promise-making side of the equation and broken it.

For this reason, I have formed "Rethink Perfect" as a counter balance for our "perfectly right" decision-making brain. It is intended to fight the effects that such thinking can have on us, especially if we are unaware of this process as we make snap decisions. "Perfectly right" has a tendency to ooze out into other parts of our thinking, on either side of "now". In my diagram below, it can even explain how we can actually achieve or touch on perfection during the day-to-day, to-ing and fro-ing, power play in a relationship. For a split second, as the power shifts to the other, we touch on this balance point or Agreement Point, in the centre.

Detail A

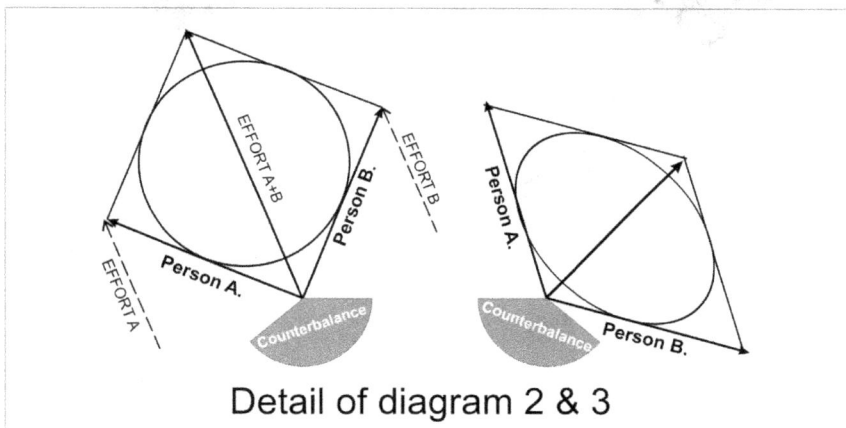

Detail of diagram 2 & 3

1. The square on the left is an ideal or cohesive relationship with the fullest area used

2. The parallelogram on the right is a compromised relationship with the area being reduced at times as in diagram 3.

An Ideal Relationship Moderated by the Rethink Perfect Moderator (Counterbalance)

Diagram 2.

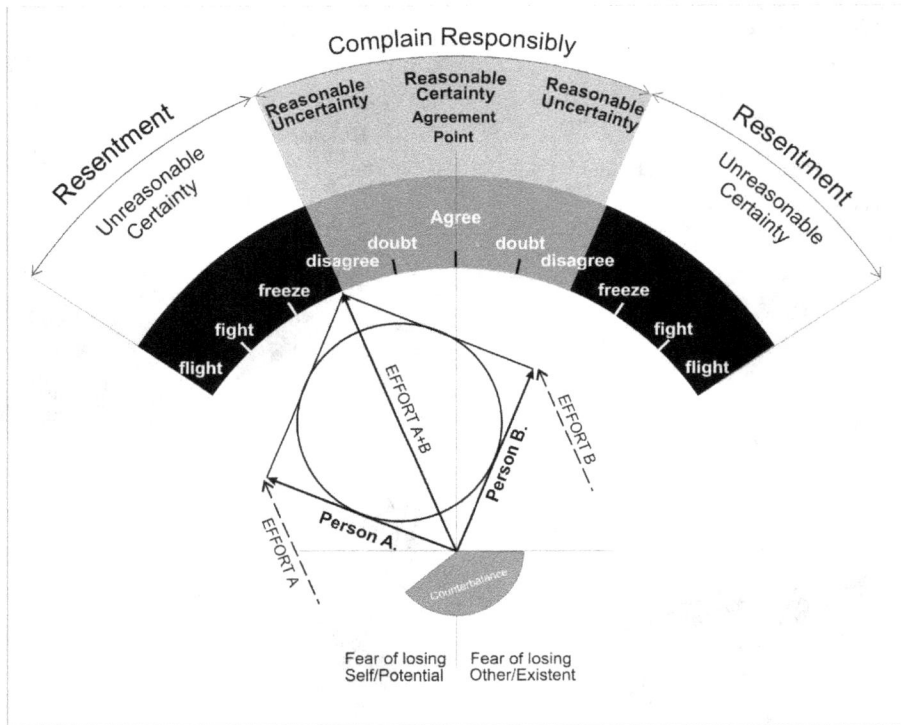

See a working model at RethinkPerfect.com

In an ideal or cohesive relationship the EFFORT A+B is greater than the individual parts ie. Person A or Person B.

A Relationship being Compromised, bypassing the Rethink Perfect Moderator (Counterbalance)

Diagram 3

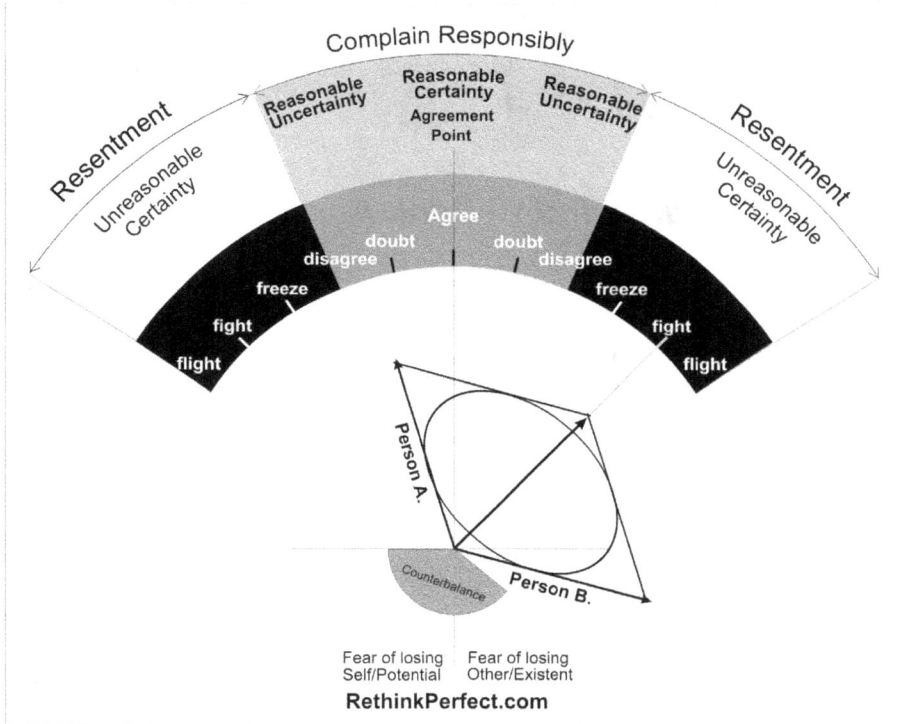

Complain Responsibly

Reasonable Uncertainty | Reasonable Certainty Agreement Point | Reasonable Uncertainty

Resentment — Unreasonable Certainty

Resentment — Unreasonable Certainty

Agree
doubt — doubt
disagree — disagree
freeze — freeze
fight — fight
flight — flight

Person A.

Counterbalance — Person B.

Fear of losing Self/Potential Fear of losing Other/Existent

RethinkPerfect.com

See working model at RethinkPerfect.com

In a heated dispute the counter balance or moderator is bypassed and the relationship deforms, contracting the area. When the two people enter into "Unreasonable Certainty" or black area and have a bitter dispute.
The goal is to keep the relationship out of this zone (black), caused by unreasonable certainty and resulting in resentment.

The relationship is literally 'growing apart' during these events.

Chapter 2 Rules and Rethink Agreements

Commitments and Compromises: I have yet to hear a guy say, "I just can't believe it, she's afraid of commitment!" This seems to be a well-worn cliché used mainly by women to describe recalcitrant men that they are trying to convert. So what is it about this word "commitment"? Commit to what? Are you committed if you only have one sexual partner in a long-term, monogamous relationship? Do you commit to the person requesting or even demanding supplication? This is a strange concept to me and, I dare say, to most males. How can we commit to a person when we both are in a state of continual flux of development and learning about ourselves and the other? I do believe in being committed - but to a concept or an agreed idea, not to the person, per se . To me, being committed to a person seems akin to being a follower or worshipper of Big Brother in George Orwell's book, *1984*. The person we are to be supposedly committed to is the equivalent to our overlord, and will ultimately become a secret enemy to be defied. Granted, for every person demanding commitment, there is someone that will be willing to promise to commit. It seems like an arms race: demanding commitment and manufacturing the promise to comply. Someone making such a "promise" is really compromising themselves, I think, to such inconsistencies expected of them. *Notice that the words *promise* and com*promise* share the same root.

Once the demand for commitment and the promise to comply are in place, they create cognitive dissonance, because the people involved have to justify this sad, compromised situation. A bastardization of the language ensues. For example, how do we reconcile our understanding that compromises are needed in relationships, while maintaining that we shouldn't compromise ourselves? What a confusion and mismatch of inconsistencies! A promise does not allow for any new information to be added into the mix of a relationship, hence a paradox occurs: once promises and commitments are in place, real and diverse conversations cease, I believe.

Being committed to a concept, however, is fine by me - so long as the concept or idea is a Rethink Idea, or Agreement. That is, open to be revisited and disputed at any time and not considered perfect or certain.

Diagram 4.

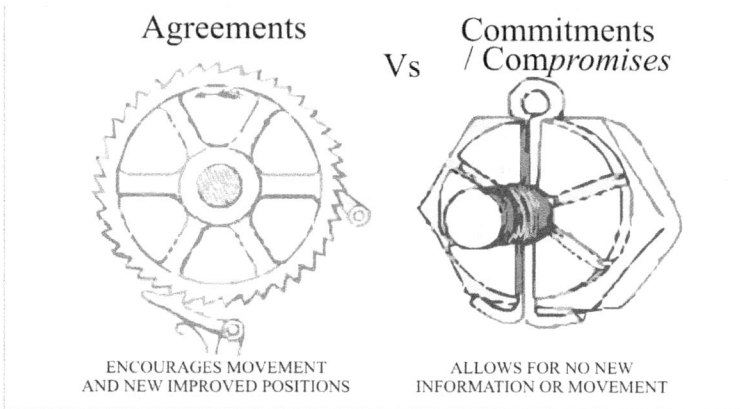

Agreements Vs Commitments / Compromises

ENCOURAGES MOVEMENT AND NEW IMPROVED POSITIONS

ALLOWS FOR NO NEW INFORMATION OR MOVEMENT

Rules

The rules of golf are a standard set of regulations and procedures by which the sport of golf should be played. They are jointly written and administered by the R&A (spun off from The Royal and Ancient Golf Club of St Andrews), the governing body of golf worldwide, except in the US. The rulebook, entitled "Rules of Golf", is published on a regular basis.

A central principle, although not one of the numbered rules, is found on the R&A rulebook's back cover:

"Play the ball as it lies, play the course as you find it, and if you cannot do either, do what is fair. But to do what is fair, you need to know the Rules of Golf."

There are over 300 **road rules** in Australia, and they are more or less standardized across the country. Obviously, the most important rules are that we drive on the left side of the road, stop at red lights, and travel at 60km on unsigned roads. Imagine a world without road rules. Probably the closest manifestation of this is to be found on inner city roads in India, where it resembles a free-for-all, with cows getting right-of-way and as a result, the traffic goes slowly and the efficiency of traveling on their roads is diminished.

Now imagine a friendship, partnership or relationship without any rules of engagement. Everything would be hit-and-miss, and we might consider ourselves very lucky to have a single lifelong friend or partner. Disputes and complaints would be the norm, not the exception. Gossip would dominate most people's conversations. Relationships would fail at a rate of approximately 50%, and the cost to society would be in the hundreds of billions annually. Conflicts, wars and the poverty they created would be ubiquitous, and the weapons used in those wars would create the biggest industry on the planet. No need to imagine this: welcome to the real world in the year 2012.

To me, having a conversation without any agreed and explicit rules of behavior is similar to having sex without discussing birth control. The former would actually help with the later. Both are referred to as "intercourse", are ubiquitous and both are an accident waiting to happen.

So, why do we not have explicit rules of engagement, which we all agree to use, for interpersonal relationships? I guess the answer is pretty simple: whatever rules we tried to institute, there would always be someone that would try exploiting them, and us. Alas, we seem to have thrown out the baby with the bath water. We also seem to be hanging onto old-fashioned and traditional relationship values that go back at least 100 years or more. It is 2012, with a world changing so fast that we are finding it difficult to keep up in most areas, yet we still are expected to "commit to someone" and "promise" to stay loyal to them for the rest of our lives, regardless of future developments. Sheah! With such inconsistent demands that we are allowing to be placed upon us, it's no wonder there is so much mental illness in the world.

Most people have their own set of standards or values and spend the rest of their lives trying to hook up with people that have a similar outlook. Rarely can a person succinctly explain what these values consist of as they are usually handed down from our parents. There are also implicit rules called manners or politeness, where a certain etiquette is assumed upon first meeting someone. The irony is that we seem to treat strangers with more respect than we do our nearest and dearest. I guess we have a lot more vested interests within our personal relationships.

When I mention the lack of common rules of engagement, most people tell me that personal relationships are all different, and that there is not one specific *way* to relate since we are all unique. I agree that if they keep saying there is no specific way, then there never will be a "way" for them or anyone in their orbit, but like the game of golf and the rules of the road, you have to start somewhere. I guess this has been the story of human development for the last few thousand years, with the rules of relating being imposed on humanity through religion, politics and philosophy. Oh, well, here we go again. Only I am merely proposing, not imposing, these rules of engagement to any willing takers. Emphasising that any agreement would only be on a trial basis and is always up for rethinking and disputing, using any of the proposed set of rules of engagement on themselves.

One of my favorite books by Edward de Bono is called *I Am Right, You Are Wrong,* where he describes parallel talking, which is when two people converse and share their thoughts. Think of two fingers standing parallel to each other. One says; "This is what I do and why (experience and/or reasoning). What do you think?" Then the other says, "Interesting, as this is what I do and why. What do you think?" And so the conversation goes, both speaking in a parallel fashion and comparing each other's concepts. Now let's look at non-parallel talking. Think of two fingers starting in parallel again. "This is what I do. What do you think?" This time he left out the reasoning and/or experience as to why he thinks it. Then the other points her finger at him saying, "No, no! You can't do that!! You have to do it this way." Then his finger also points: "What? Don't tell me what to do!" And so the conversation spirals out of control, with both desiring to be right, and thinking that the other is wrong. "Your full of shit!"

My book is partly based on Parallel Talking and the agreed rules needed to get there and stay nearby. It's a way to get back to the two fingers standing in parallel together, sharing their thoughts. And like the fingers, the two people's shared thoughts can stand or fall simply by reason. If they stand, they stand; if they fall, they fall. They don't need us to point our fingers at them. Having confidence in this principle, that is, confidence enough to just try, is the beginning of the Rethink Perfect agreement process. Our attempts speaking much louder than our silence.

But what happens if one of us goes back to pointing our finger at the other? How do we protest or dispute without also pointing our finger? Well, this is where we are going to need an agreed-upon process or rules of engagement. For starters, I am proposing six concepts, all beginning with the letter A, that I think can achieve this process and bring us back to parallel talking. More on the six concepts in Chapter 5.

But first let's agree what Rethink Agreements and disagreements are: I propose that to achieve this process we will need to use the following definitions:

- "Agreement" = what you *and* I consider acceptable to us, for now.
- "Disagreement" = what you *or* I consider unacceptable to us, for now.

These definitions are only related to interpersonal interactions, and do not take into account any legal and binding contract definitions for agreements.

If we can allow these two definitions of Rethink Agreements and disagreements to stand for now, we can move on to Chapter 3 to try them out.

Chapter 3 Complain Responsibly

Exactly what is a complaint? As simple as this question may sound, I think that most people will not be able to answer it successfully. Is it a problem that we did not foresee? An action that has led to our resentment? The playwright Bertolt Brecht said that as soon as something seems the most obvious thing in the world, it means that we have abandoned all attempts to understand it. I think we may have done this with words like complain, conversation, commitment, certainty, promises, agreements, love, respect and many, many more concepts that we take for granted. Sir Ken Robinson talks about taking things for granted in his book *The Element*:

"One of the key principles of the Element is that we need to challenge what we take for granted about our abilities and the abilities of other people. This isn't as easy as one might imagine. Part of the problem with identifying the things we take for granted is that we don't know what they are because we take them for granted in the first place. They become basic assumptions that we don't question, part of the fabric of our logic. We don't question them because we see them as fundamental, as an internal part of our lives. Like air. Or gravity. Or Oprah."

What is the purpose of a complaint? Is there a responsible procedure that we can agree to use? Is it an expression to ensure that we can avoid the issue in the future? Surely then the most responsible complaint I ever make would be to avoid the problem in the first place? Maybe! More in this later.

I think that we were born to complain. From the moment we first opened out mouth we were complaining about something. Learning to do it responsibly is the life time goal.

Resentment is not a complaint! I think it is the result of not complaining responsibly and making sure that the problem never occurred in the first place. It is the internal frustration at being stupid enough to allow such problems to occur in the first place. Resentment does not solve the problem that complaining responsibly can, and may result in revenge. As the saying goes, "If you go down the path of revenge, take two coffins".

So what can we do to avoid slipping into resentment? Having rules of engagement to prevent the complaint from ever occurring in the first place would be a good and proactive start. Failing to have any agreements in place, at this point, all I can suggest is that you apologise for participating in the conversation or relationship without such terms and suggest that if you are to continue relating with them that you work at getting some.

If you do have some terms or rules of engagement in place then I suggest you go direct to the source of your problem in person. Having such agreements in place will facilitate this direct approach. Simply voice your complaint, and present all of your evidence. Offer an apology for not dealing with the issue as swiftly as you could have and get an acceptable apology from the alleged perpetrator so that you can feel confident that, from now on, the problem will be less likely to recur.

Despite our best efforts, failures will occur when we try making responsible complaints. I mean, we can't be expected to complain perfectly responsibly, can we? Most complaints don't reach their intended, rightful recipient; that is, the person or organisation the objection should be directed at. And if it does reach the target, it is not delivered in the same format in which it first started out. Usually, it arrives weeks later, compounded by numerous other complaints, demands, frustrations, resentment, and lack of appreciation. This is especially true for business, but also true for interpersonal relations. If you are on the receiving end of criticism, you may be the last to hear it. If we could only hear complaints before they began making the rounds behind our backs, we would be blessed with a plethora of feedback and pertinent information that we could use to modify our behavior, or at least to start addressing the situation.

Breadcrumbs: One way we seem to send and receive complaints is through "breadcrumbs" or cryptic messages that we are supposed to decipher in order to figure out what the problem is. A good start, but I am suggesting a more responsible method.

If you doubt what I am saying, eavesdrop on conversations around you when at cafes or on the street. I'm reasonably certain you will find the dialogue consists of countless complaints of unfulfilled desires. However, they are not delivered to the ears of the person, government, or business that they are claiming created the problem.

So how do we change this entrenched culture? Should we even recognize such behavior as a problem that needs changing at all? This book is an attempt to expose what I consider to be an obvious problem, and to suggest a number of solutions and tools that could turn this behavior around. I think that it has been so long since we have disclosed our complaints responsibly to the rightful recipients that we have forgotten how it is done. Most of us already seem certain of the response if we were to apply the direct approach.

At the same time, we seem to have forgotten how to hear such direct approaches and dissenting information. We have to change how we deliver complaints and how we receive them.

Rethink Perfect is the story of my personal journey to rediscover the art of complaining responsibly, of how I learned to dissect the two skills of giving and receiving complaints, and of my attempts to apply responsible complaints to my own behavior.

When you think about it, it is pretty obvious that it is not what we have in common that causes our relationships to disintegrate, but what we don't have in common that provokes our unresolved disputes. But where can we find information that shows the "proper" way to deliver this information to our intended? How do we go about airing our complaints so that we can get a constructive and balanced outcome for all? Where is the dialogue amongst our peers and elders reminding us that the direct approach is the best way? Who will give us the tools that we should use to deliver and hear the messages that are most difficult to give and to receive?

What if I told you that there is a long lost method detailed in the bible? (Now, don't worry, I am not about to bible bash you. Rethink Perfect has no ties with God or Jesus. I only reference this verse like any other paragraph of interest that I have stumbled upon over my 52 years.) This paragraph is less than 10 lines long, but does seem to summarizes what I call complaining responsibly about someone or an organisation that we have a problem with.

Go directly to the source of your complaint:

In Matthew *ch. 18, i*n plain English: If you have an issue with someone,

1. Go to that person alone to discuss and try to resolve it. If successful you have regained a friend.

2. If unsuccessful, then try again with a witness or two, and establish each person's argument or point of view.

3. If still unsuccessful, take the dispute before your peer group, family or whatever organisation or section you both belong to, for an open hearing from each person.

4. If still unsuccessful, then it is time to part company with them. (Somehow I doubt it would ever get as far as this)

Now some people might say, "What if it is a small issue?" I say that if you cannot resolve a "small" issue, then what chance have you got to resolve a big issue in the future? It is now becoming more apparent to me that Rethink Perfect is built around this method of conversing. That is being willing to test my complaint to the point where my peers can judge it and form their recommendations. This simple and long lost method of complaining to each other directly and listening to complaints will allow us to change and improve our disputes so much more effectively than we are now doing. No more sweeping so-called "small issues" under the carpet.

If you look at how we process our legal complaints, the legal system pretty much encompasses this verse. But applying such a process in our interpersonal relations would be a very interesting approach, and possibly reduce a lot of legal processes and save millions of dollars if such a system were used.

Let's assume that we have agreed that we need to deal directly with the people and organisations with which we had problems. Our next step would be to agree on a process of sharing our complaints, so that we could get some satisfaction. Chapter 5, explains my proposed process to complain responsibly. That is my proposed six rules of engagement for such a forum.

If you lose it (your cool) we've lost it (the plot):
I was talking to a woman recently, and I told her about a poem that I wrote some 30 years ago when I was 21. It went something like this:

My knowledge of women is but a speck,
and that's because they're extraterrestrials, I expect.
My fear of them is something I don't lack,
and that's because of their habit to attack........

She questioned my line about women's "habit to attack", so I asked her if she knew any women that did not become aggressive? In return, she wondered whether I knew any men that did not get aggressive? I agreed, but countered that we all know that a man's aggression is unacceptable, whereas I have found that most women seem to justify their aggression by blaming men.

I think it is time for us to agree that all anger and aggression, whether from men or women, is unacceptable. Understandable, yes, because we are human (imperfect) - but not acceptable. Further, we agree that we cannot blame the other person for our choice to get angry or aggressive. It's time to rethink our *habit* to attack and become more accountable for such unacceptable behavior.

Interestingly, losing our cool does not usually happen in a vacuum. In a conversation, it is up to each of us to keep an eye on the tempo. It is also our responsibility to have in place an agreed upon process for dealing with the possibility of losing it.

Complaining responsibly is about getting these fundamental ground rules understood *before* we start. Now, of course, I could be wrong about this; but after much contemplation and 52 years of NOT living by this rule, I believe that this is the way forward for me. It is what I like, and how I desire to be treated. Losing our cool and trying to convert each other are closely linked, I think. As the saying goes, "Familiarity breeds contempt". The more familiar we are to each other, the more we seem to want to convert the other. So then maybe it is more that "Contempt breeds familiarity" - i.e., conformity and lack of diversity out of fear of the other's contempt for us.

The Rethink Agreements and the six rules of engagement (see Ch 5) have been designed to allow us to prepare for our aggressive failures, and to catch each other before we lose it.

Having a clear plot helps us to not lose our cool, I think. What is your plot? Mine is to convert my concepts by incorporating your feedback, so that we may reach an agreement and a possible solution - without losing my cool or yours.

Compromised Relationship: It is all very well to say we shouldn't get angry or lose our cool but sometimes, if we are pushing each other's boundaries of understanding, we can push too hard and risk compromising ourselves and the relationship. At this point, we need to be prepared for such a failure and have an agreed method to dissipate or moderate such behavior before or when it happens so that we come back to diagram 2. of an ideal or cohesive relationship. Overestimating our relationship rather than underestimating it, I believe that we are going to get the most from it, but at the same time stress it.

By agreeing that aggression or losing our cool is understandable but not acceptable, we can develop tools to deal with this. Trying to be rational during this period when we are in the black zone is not very easy, so it is best for us to be aware of the signs that we are heading for a compromised situation, and deal with the signs and our behavior before we lose it further. In other words, get some agreed rules of engagement, in preparation for such failures.

"I failed my way to success" Thomas Edison

Chapter 4 Prepare for the Failure

It's uncanny how many people perceive the title of this chapter as being negative. To "prepare for the failure", to me, is to prepare for the reality of life and to deal with it. Life is full of failures or failings. From the moment we first try to stand up (and fall) as a baby, to our first business startup or our first kiss, we are destined to fail before we succeed. Being prepared for such failures can reduce the pain and go a long way towards preventing or reducing our next one. To prepare for a bush fire, tsunami or earthquake would not be perceived as being negative. To have a spare parachute as a skydiver or taking our car for a service is being proactive in our thinking, and entails being aware of the potential for failure. So why is it that when it comes to relationships, we do not prepare for the failure and worse still, why do we see such preparations as unnecessary, unproductive and negative in outlook? Rethink Perfect is intended to answer these questions and shine some light on the consequences of a lack of preparation for failure. As Benjamin Franklin (and Winston Churchill) put it, "By failing to prepare, you are preparing to fail."

Prepare for the Failure: How do we prepare for all the possible failures that might occur in relationships? It is inevitable that we will fall short when trying to explain how we would like to be treated within a relationship. After all, these are new thoughts and feelings, and we need practice to be able to share them. Of course this book could be another one of those failed attempts, and it is no doubt riddled with errors and inconsistencies that could stand improvement. However, it is through this understanding of our fallibility and preparation for it that we are more likely to be proactive rather than reactive to failures within a relationship. I have said before that I think the people that talk about the merits of hindsight are far less likely to use their foresight. That is it is much easier to explain why something failed after the fact than to predict the failure before. It is this underutilized foresight or awareness of our potential to fail while in a relationship, and the uncertainty this can bring, that I am hoping to address throughout this book.

Now some of you may say that my focus is too much on the negative effects of failure, and others may say that I am planning for the perfect relationship. Either way, hold that thought and try to rethink it, and maybe we will end up close to the centre of them both. Either way, I am bound to fail most of the time, as I doubt that I will touch on, for long, a perfect balance between the two poles. I think we get frustrated and aggressive with a person when we expect perfect action from them; reciprocal aggression makes the other not much different. Getting an agreement to help each other out of our unreasonable expectations or certitude is paramount before moving forward in a relationship, I think. Otherwise, it is death by a thousand expectations of perfection.

Growing Apart: Ask someone today why their relationship failed and they will usually come back with the well-worn cliché "We grew apart". Saying that we grew apart, I think, is akin to saying, "It fell out of the sky!" when asked, "Why did the plane crash?" Of course you grew apart, and of course the plane fell out of the sky, but why? Rethink Perfect is my attempt to plan the perfect relationship by explaining why failures occur in relationships, and is based on my own personal experience in an experimental relationship that I entered into specifically to test my theories on love and relationships; theories that I had to completely rethink afterwards, and an experience that has allowed me to "data mine" over the last twelve years, so as to redevelop Rethink Perfect. It is also based on studying my brother's personal relationship with his partner, which lasted for ten years, and on his personal participation in acting as a sounding board for my concepts. And finally, all the hundreds of conversations I have had with people who have experienced failed relationships and the failures within their relationship, (no shortage there), have contributed to this thesis.

Now, some of you also may ask, "Why not focus on the over 50% 'successful' relationships instead of the failed ones?" A good point, but who can tell how successful a relationship really is? It is what goes on behind closed doors that is very hard to observe, as we all strive to keep up appearances. At least with failed relationships, there is much more transparency, as it is pretty hard to hide. My favorite question used to be to ask divorcees whose fault the demise of the relationship was, and on most occasions they would point their finger at the other and say "30/70" or "40/60". This gave me an insight into one possible reason for why the relationship failed. I have always said that we are not the victim of the person that we choose to be with, but the victim of our own choice. No point in blaming anyone else for my failed relations. I prefer a 50/50 point of view. As my dear old mum says, "You make your bed, you lie in it".

Positive and Negative, Failure and Success: So why do we see "preparing for the failure" as a negative? Well, it could be due to a number of reasons, but the age of so-called "positive thinking" probably has a lot to do with it. Also, religion has contributed to this form of thinking. For example, if things go well for us, it was because of our god and that we pleased him; if things fail, it was because we have displeased him. In reality, the probability of us succeeding or failing is directly linked to how well or not that we prepared. The rest is just superstition with a degree of luck thrown in for good measure. How we deal with chance or luck and the language we use also contributes to this thinking. We seem to live by false dichotomies. That is, good and bad, right and wrong, success and failure, with very little nuance in between. If we are not successful, then are we failures? Or if a business is not a failure, then is it a success? Don't worry, I am not saying that I am immune from this form of thinking. I am writing from experience as an ex-born again Christian from '83 to '85, who has finally seen the light or is seeing the light a bit more clearly; (I was actually kicked out of the organisation for questioning their dogma).

Failure and success are mere concepts, and this chapter will give you my slant on these concepts and how they affect relationships. First thing to realise is that it is not "our" failure, it is the systems, processes and their parts we chose to use, or that are around us, that fail. It is not "our fault", it is a fault of these systems and parts that we chose. Heck, when you think about it, we don't even fail when we die, it is just that our heart, lungs or other body parts fail. Preparing for these failures, by looking after our heart, lungs and body, generally can keep us alive longer. We don't need to blame anyone or any one thing for the failure, we just need to prepare for how we choose the system's parts and processes around us so that we get less failing parts, less often. Failure is not personal. It does not have a conscience. It doesn't happen because we are good people or bad people. It happens for a number of reasons, one of them being our lack of preparation. It is not god that kept it from failing, or the devil that made it fail. We just need to choose to be more prepared for the failure, and choose well.

Fear of Failure: There are not too many people that have not heard about the negative effects of fear. But what is fear? Fear is what keeps us alive. Fear of dying, fear of pain and discomfort. Fear of confusion and fear of not knowing or uncertainty. Then we have irrational fears such as paranoia and various phobias. And then we come to fear of failure. My definition of fear of failure is broken up into two parts:

1. **Fear to lose other** i.e. fear of losing what we have or think we have (Existent).
2. **Fear of losing self** i.e. fear of losing our future time and energy (Potential).

36

To me these are quite legitimate fears, but do need to be understood and executed with this knowledge and awareness. If we fail to prepare and gain such understanding, we are likely to allow our two fears of failure to affect us in a more negative way rather than a more positive one. See diagram 7 on page 41. Understanding what part Reasonable Uncertainty plays in our relationships can help us control our fear of loss and stop us going over to Unreasonable Certainty. In a relationship, an awareness of our two fears of failure or loss can help keep us more often in the grey zone and away from the black zone.

Rethink Perfect is about realising that *we* don't fail, but we may have failed thoughts and attempts. The language we use to describe failure is part of the systems or processes that can lead to failures. If after reading this book, you fail to increase your preparations and understandings of failure, it will be due to my failure to convert my concepts into agreements with you.

So, why do we seem to assume that the word "failure" is associated with the person? Why is it that we are so quick to label someone that has not achieved their goal a "failure", rather than identifying the systems or processes that we used that were responsible for the failure? I guess that is an easy question to answer. It takes work to analyze what went wrong and why, and work means energy and time. Fundamentally, I suppose we all want to conserve time and energy, especially if it is our own, following the path of least resistance, once again. It seems that the unreasonable certainty of blaming and labeling others, instead of examining ourselves and how we look at failure, can be seen as the simplest and easiest way. One of the most common responses I have experienced while I have been trying to convert my ideas has been that I "think too much", as though there is a set level of how much we should or shouldn't think and they are the authors of this. More shades of 1984, me thinks.

Rethink Perfect, is about how we can prepare for failure between people at work, in business or relationships by identifying and understanding these processes. It is not about simply generalising and using clichés, by saying that "we have to communicate more". This is as broad a statement as saying "we need to fix the engine" when a plane crashes. It is more about identifying the key part/s of the systems and processes that we use during communication in relationships (adjustable language and agreements, for example) or inside the workings of the engine (fuel filter redesign, for example). It is the preparations that we suggest as possible fixes, appreciating the possibilities of certain weaknesses and doing something about them before they occur, to prevent the ultimate failure of the relationship or plane (commonly called preventative maintenance).

It will be the failures that occur when testing out your new procedures that are ultimately going to help you learn to understand what caused them and how to prepare for future failures.

Phase Transition
What is a "phase transition" and how does it apply to relationships?

Diagram 5

See Video on RethinkPerfect.com

A phase transition is what **Michael J. Mauboussin** refers to in his book *Think Twice*, when talking about the millennium bridge "failure" or design flaw. The bridge was designed and built with a flaw, so that when more than 165 people crossed it at the same ime, the bridge began to oscillate from side to side. When only 155 people were on the bridge, the movement was not so noticeable. It was this phase of adding just 10 people that created this extreme phase transition.

Diagram 6

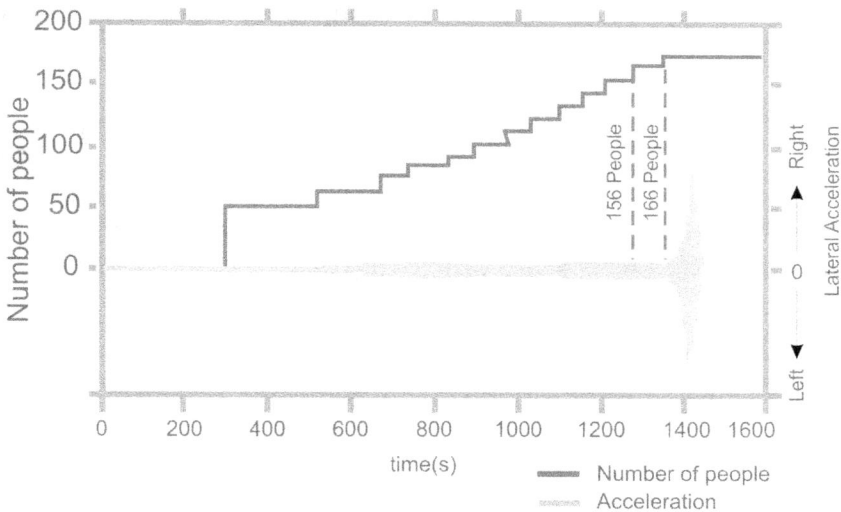

Another example of a phase transition in nature is the transformation of water into its various states. We could also use the analogies of the "straw that broke the camel's back" or "the last straw".

Well, we all know that this happens in relationships too, don't we? How many times have we heard the loud and unpleasant screech, "I'm sick of this"? We may have engaged in the same behavior five times previously without hearing a peep, but just one more time and bam! we're supposedly in trouble.

Phase transitions are used to explain and predict catastrophic failure that can occur, such as an economist might use to prepare for a crash in the stock market. I am using phase transitions to explain the point that a conversation goes from an efficient sharing of information in "synergy" ie. follows the view that a cohesive relationship is greater than the sum of its parts. To a heated dispute, where the contracting relationship is less than the sum of the parts. See diagram 7.

I guess anyone that is separated or divorced will understand the concept of phase transition. One day you are there, and the next day you're not, and you find yourself wondering how your relationship got to this point without you realising you were headed for a fall.

So, what caused the phase transition of the millennium bridge? Simple. As the bridge began to sway, the people on it widened their strides to counter the oscillation. They unintentionally did this in unison with the oscillation, which created even more sideways motion until it became extreme.

It was their "coordinated behavior" or lack of diversity in movement that created the problem in the system (and the design that was not prepared for such behavior failure). It is the same lack of diversity that can occur in relationships, which can eventually tip it over into a phase transition. The failure to speak up enough and inject diverse thinking into the relationship, instead of making it more secure, can in actual fact set it up for a catastrophic failure, over time.

How we inject and receive our diverse views (complaints), so that our dissent is accepted and ultimately agreed to, is what Rethink Perfect is about and follows from the previous chapter of Complaining Responsibly.

This phase transition in a relationship might be when it is stressed to the point that it deforms, contracting the area of the parallelogram, as in the following diagram, going from Reasonable Uncertainty to Unreasonable Certainty:

Diagram 7

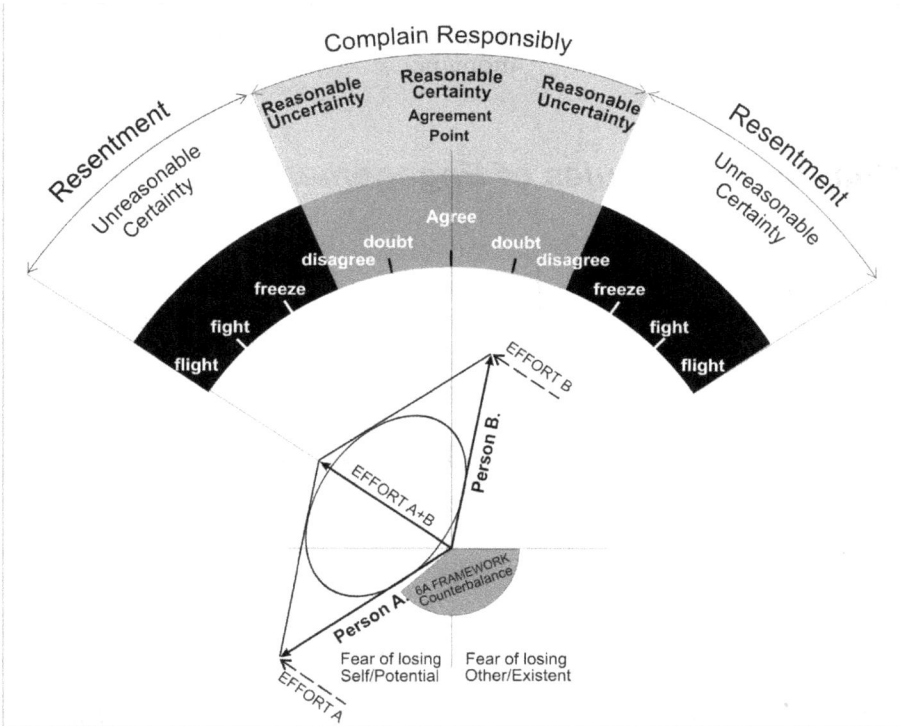

The effects of unreasonable certainty (black zone) and how it deforms and contracts the area of the relationship. The 6A Framework or Moderator is still present but has been bypassed. "Freezing" of staying silence is the first indicator of the phase transition.

The overall effort achieved, EFFORT A+B, is less than the individual parts of Person A or Person B.

In an ideal or cohesive relationship, the EFFORT A+B is greater than the individual parts or Persons. See diagram 2 on page 17.

"I don't believe in equality, I believe in quality equality"
Anonymous

Chapter 5 Six Rules of Engagement

I have found through trial and error, and over the course of some 26 years, that making a Rethink Agreement, however flawed, is a good start for improving behavior, and also for improving previous and less than perfect agreements. In order to begin sharing our complaints in a responsible manner, and to put us on the path of creating even better agreements, I think we need to first agree to the following six rules of engagement. The goal is to try to achieve Parallel Talking, as mentioned in Ch. 1, and to try to get back to that point whenever we stray off track in the heat of participating in a "real" conversation.

Now as simple and reasonable that these behavioral rules may sound, to actually get working agreements in place has not been so easy. I guess being accountable has a two edged sword. It may protect us from abuse but it also stops us from abusing others. Ultimately it is our choice.

Speaking: These agreements are based on the Golden Rule: treating others the way we would like to be treated. So, how do I like to be treated, or more to the point, how do I not want to be treated? Not such a simple question to be answered, I have found. I am still working this out, and probably will be for the rest of my life. What I have found is that I do not like people using non-adjustable language with me, which is when they set themselves up as some omnipotent authority on life by being all-knowing and certain. There was an apt quote by Dr. Who in the show called 'Midnight', (series 4): "I'm glad you've got an absolute definition of life in the Universe, but perhaps the Universe has got ideas of its own, hmm?" I also found that it irks me when people use non-accountable language with me; that's when they try to blame me or someone else for how they choose to live and feel. And finally I found that high volume, a harsh tone, and aggressive language are not acceptable to me. I concluded that if this was how I did not want to be treated, then maybe I could try treating others with *Adjustable*, *Accountable* and *Acceptable* (to them) language.

Respond/Dispute: So the question arose: how was I going to treat someone when they did not treat me with Adjustable, Accountable and Acceptable language? Through more trial and error, I have discovered that a good start is made by first *Appreciating* their contribution and participation, however flawed. Better for someone to speak with me and make a mistake than not to say something and seem flawless. To *Acknowledge* what they were trying to achieve was also useful, I found that I hated being ignored. Finally, I found an *Apology* for exposing their flaw and not delivering my message so perfectly and early enough, during this process could get me over the line to encourage them to use more Adjustable, Accountable and ultimately more Acceptable language. This is the method I have tested on my brother and me and have gotten some pretty good results.

The best option was having both participants agree beforehand to these two delivery concepts of speaking and responding. My ultimate goal or Holy Grail is to try to achieve a constructive conversation without these rules agreed to beforehand, if possible. But for now, here is my more detailed proposal for these rules of engagement that I am hoping to get your agreement on.

Detail of Speaking Rules: Are that we agree to try to speak using the following language:

1. Adjustable: We agree to try use Adjustable language when we are conversing, complaining or trying to make our point. Examples of this include reminding each other that these are only our opinions and prefacing our statements with "I think..." or "to me", etc. There is no room for absolute language, such as "I know", "it can't be done" or "that's impossible" without these prefaces, at least. At any point, we can enquire if the other person is still speaking from opinion rather than from fact, or using Factive Verbs.

In the book Simpleology the author, Mark Joyner refers to Alfred Korzybski, who pioneered General Semantics.

"In his seminal work "Science and Sanity," Alfred Korzybski attempts to break down and analyse this relationship between language and reality. Korzybski recognized that our defective mental model could potentially cause serious behavioural dysfunction and felt strongly that this was rooted in the inherent nature of our language".

"Korzybski felt that much of the problem was our inadequate and unhealthy use of the verb "to be". Simple "is" statements only make sense when you deal in absolutes. But it would seem that absolutes are rarely (if ever) adequate for describing the world."

General Semantics included some rules such as the use of "To me..." and other caveats to deal with such absolute statements.

2. Accountable: Being accountable in that we take responsibility for what we say or do, rather than **blaming** others. For example, "You make me so frustrated" changes to "I get frustrated when we talk about this". No room for victims and persecutors. We make our bed and we lie in it. To me, **rhetorical** questions are used when we are not willing to be accountable for our thought or argument and use the question so we do not have to follow up with a reason or explain our lack of experience. "Why do you do it that way?", can be converted to "I don't think you should do it that way", which would then require an explanation from the speaker as to why. The speaker then becomes accountable for what they think and say. Finally when we propose a statement we are responsible to provide our **reasoning**, data (experience). It is not up to others to do our work. For us to be accountable we need to provide some level of evidence, first. Finally, being able to simply admit that we were wrong when in fact we were.

3. Acceptable: If we find something that was said that we did not like for any reason, or even if we were unsure as to why, we do not have to accept it. If we notice any inconsistency or aggression in the other's tone, we can simply say so, hopefully sooner rather than later, by using the following three speaking tools.

Detail of Responding (disputing) Rules: Are that we agree to try to respond using the following language:

4. Appreciate their contribution, remembering that it is difficult to converse and create in a vacuum. Expecting to hear what we consider to be perfection is unrealistic.

5. Acknowledge the context of their last point that was made and what they are trying to achieve. Ignoring them and their point is not an option. In fact, to me the word is the ugliest sounding word in the English language; IG-NORE.

6. Apologise or explain to them how you would prefer to be spoken to, and why you think that would be of benefit to them. An example of this would be: "Thanks for letting me know about this issue, but I am sorry I don't agree with your delivery. Can you talk to me in a more adjustable (accountable or acceptable) way so that I can help you? (give you more constructive feedback on your complaint)"

This is the basis of the Dispute Moderator: how we relate with each other as we try to disprove and improve both these concepts and our general knowledge. We do this by conversing and sharing complaints. By outsourcing someone else's ears and thoughts and vice versa, we have an opportunity to increase our capacity for learning and understanding every time we converse. This is a process we have been unconsciously trying to achieve for millennia on a hit-and-miss basis, I would say. Bitter disputes or overly polite discussions are the evidence of this ongoing process. By having an agreed method to moderate our disputes allows us to continue such real and valuable conversations.

Eventually, we end up with what I call The Agreement Matrix or Dispute Moderator. These rules allow us to begin our Rethink Perfect conversations and actually test our six agreements during the process, to see if they fail and need reviewing in light of the differing contexts and improved understandings. This is my plan for perfect relations AND the preparations for the failure. When your next conversation ends up in an argument or aggressive dispute, just think back and see if you can spot the times that you or they did not use one or more of the 6A framework. Then apologise and start over. Or better still, get the Dispute Moderator agreed to beforehand, test it out and send me your feedback as to its effectiveness.

*Note: Acceptable Vs Acceptance: Most spiritual books will talk about the need for acceptance and that we should accept what other people say and feel. I have never read or heard a reason why they believe this. But compare this with Rethink Perfect and it is almost an opposite approach. That we do not "need" or "have to" accept what is said if we do not like it. That, what we choose to accept needs to be in an acceptable form, to us. That is; tone, volume, content and overall delivery. And if we are not happy we can thank them for their efforts and request that they try again.

Rethink Perfect Dispute Moderator
(6A Framework or Six Rules of Engagement)

Diagram 8.

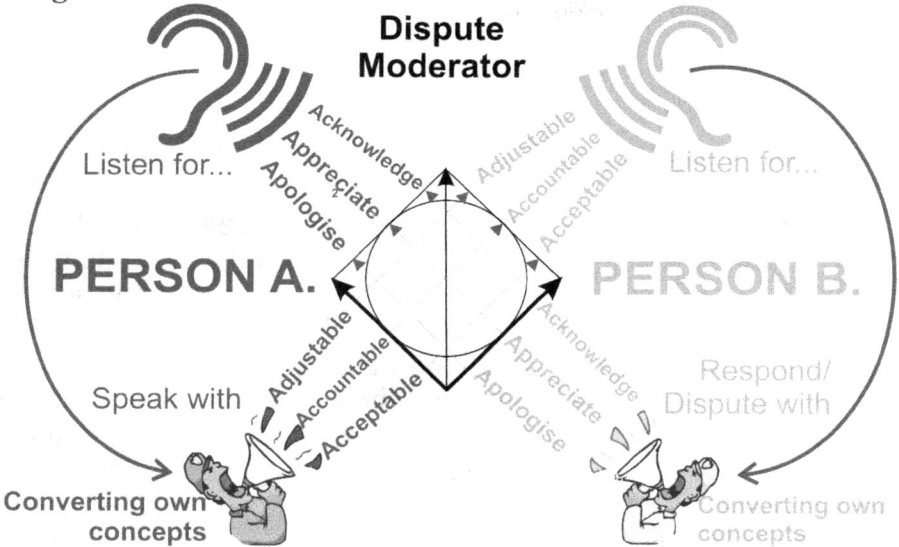

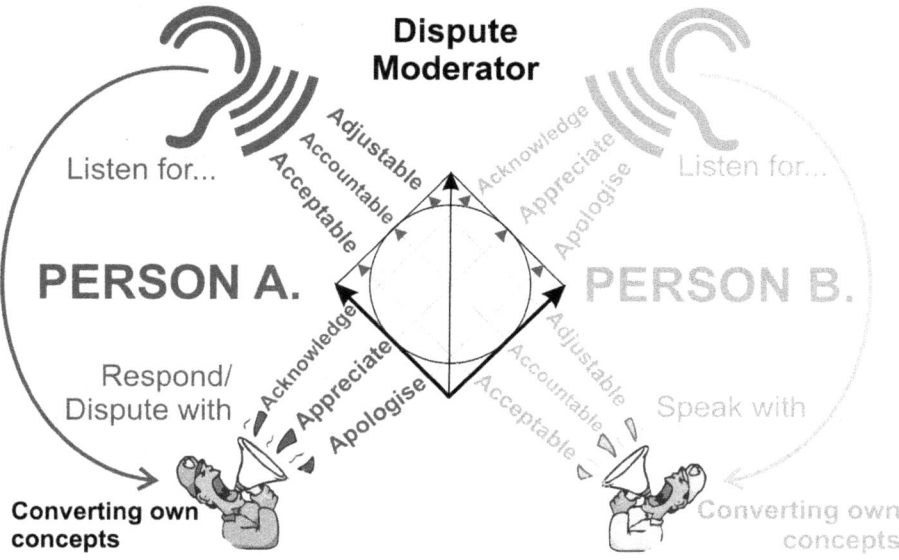

"If everyone is thinking alike, then somebody isn't thinking".
George S. Patton

Chapter 6 Conversations and Conversions

"True Conversing" - The Long Lost Treasure: People don't "truly converse" anymore, unless it is for work, business, on TV or in political forums. But one-on-one conversing seems to have disappeared. So what do we have in its place? Well, people pretend to agree, while smiling obsequiously. They may nod and say "yes" or "absolutely" when they are unsure or are thinking "no" - but refrain from sharing their converse opinion one-on-one for fear of disagreement and possible conflict.

This is what conversation is to me. Not chit chat, small talk or gossip, but con-ver-sation, as in "conversely speaking" or "on the converse".

So where has conversing gone? Heck, when I point out what I think conversing is really for, some look at me dumbfounded, as though I were speaking a different language.

I think that we have collectively spent so long in this non-conversing state that if/when this conversing takes place, it ends up much more in conflict, as an argument or bitter dispute, than an actual conversation or discourse. Most people seem to be out of practice and have forgotten the rules of engagement. Many have never learned them in the first place. I have to admit I am not in much better shape and could do with a lot more practice.

How long has this been going on? For too long!

And since there is very little real conversation, it is no wonder there are so many failed marriages, conflict with workmates, and generally no relationship that I have ever aspired to emulate, save one. Lacking a forum to air grievances, makes complaining or adding constructive criticism difficult, without the fear of the situation escalating out of our control. Abuse becomes a real possibility in most people's minds, and discourages them from what I call "conversing" or contributing real and honest feedback.

From the Start: In 1988 I asked a young woman I worked with what she thought a conversation was for. Startled by the question, she told me that she thought that I was f#%ked, but in a nice sort of way. We both had a giggle and talked about something else. But I was serious at the time, and had pondered the answer to such a question for some years previously, although I had never actually put it into words. After asking the question, I was off to a flying start and from then on, I kept an eye out for an answer to such a simple, yet important, thought. Only now, some 23 years on, I consider I have an answer that could change my world.

Conversations and Conversions: I guess one of the reasons that this journey has been so time consuming and difficult for me is that agreements and conversations are so inextricably linked. To convert better agreements, we need better conversations; and to achieve better conversations, we need to convert better agreements. Also, it wasn't until I truly acquired my semantic meaning of "conversation" that I could move forward with my quest.

When I looked at "conversation" in the context of such terms as "on the converse" and "conversely speaking", I found a key. The meaning of these terms is that we come from opposite positions and exchange conflicting concepts. From this position, I have taken conversation to mean that we aim to *convert* our own concepts so that we get a *convergence* of ideas or a *conversion* that we call agreements and from that, possible solutions to our problems. Our goal being to make this an ongoing and evolving process for the duration of the relationship. This was a real breakthrough for me and my brother, Steve. It showed us how to approach conversation, especially with the emphasis on aiming to convert our *own* concepts and not the other's.

Converting Our Own Concepts, not Other People's:
Recently Steve and I made an agreement that we would only convert our own concepts and not each other's. I think the reason that we have a conversation is to convert. Not to convert people or their ideas, but to convert our own concepts through other's feedback, and to get agreements.

I have a feeling that this is the keystone or foundation that can make a relationship work smoothly. I believe that most people try to convert the other person and their concepts as well as their own concepts. In fact, Steve admitted as much to me when I asked him what he thought conversation was for. I think I was guilty of this also. By mutually agreeing not to try to convert each other's concepts, it allows us a point of reference if either one of us breaches our agreement. Trying to influence the other's behavior creates a conversation feedback loop, with both of us trying to convert the other, and an argument or fight subsequently occurs. The more we try to achieve conversion of the other, the more problems we have during the conversation.

Trying to convert only our own concepts, so that the other person can understand and agree with them, takes much more time and effort, and also a belief that it is possible, but I think the results are more beneficial in the long term. This takes an agreement, as well as the discipline to delay our gratification. Trying to convert or convince the other is an attempt to remove dissent and diversity in their thinking, and it produces conformity and clones through acquiescence especially when coercion is used.

It has taken me over 26 years to get to this point. Having this agreement in place with Steve should help us get along better, I think. We'll see.

Finally, I think the key to a fruitful conversation is to be willing to always consider the other person's feedback, especially if we do not agree with it. Once again, this encourages diverse views by raising questions and answers that we may not have considered before, and allows us to refine our own concepts even further, rather than focusing on trying to convert or convince them.

Disprove and Improve Our Own Concepts: As much as I think it is our job to convert our own concepts it is also our job to disprove our own concepts. I did not include "prove", as I believe that it is unlikely that I ever could, with any certainty, which is what Karl Popper endorsed. He promoted the thought that no theory can be proved, only disproved. As to be proved as a certainty we would have to know all available information and even the unavailable stuff. It is not my job to disprove your concept any more than it is to convert it. You look after your concepts, I look after mine. You disprove your concepts and I disprove mine. When we state our position in a conversation, we are responsible for also stating our reasoning and/or provide any data (experience) for why we think so. We can then simply compare results with anyone that has differing reasoning and experiences that form their concepts. This is similar to the parallel type talking that I mentioned before in chapter 2.

Black Swan Thinking: In the 16th century it was believed that there were only white swans and the black swan was used in an idiom similar to the saying "as rare as hens teeth" or in this case, "a rare bird in the lands, and very like a black swan." Both were presumed not to exist. That is teeth in hens and black swans. That was before Europeans visited Australia where we only have black swans. After that they had to drop that idiom.

Nassim Nicholas Taleb wrote his book on the subject in 2007 called The Black Swan. Taleb regards almost all major scientific discoveries, historical events, and artistic accomplishments as "black swans"—undirected and unpredicted. The irony is that some people like to believe in facts or certainty, until disproven. Usually referring to "hindsight" and its benefits. Unfortunately, it seems that no matter how many times this "Black Swan" thinking is exposed as a fallacy, its users continue to believe in such, so called facts or certainty. Rethink Perfect thinking opposes this type of certitude and I say that people that refer to power of hindsight as an excuse for not being aware of the unknown, have little desire to use their foresight to try.

Conversing and Creativity on Steroids: I started out on this quest to discover a better way to relate, but in the process I may have also discovered a better way to create or convert concepts. In the past, creative movements such as the Bauhaus, Impressionism, Heidelberg School, The Manhattan Project and the Apollo Programs were created out of a desire to achieve a single goal. Find a goal, preferably an inspirational one, that will harness peoples' ego in their quest to achieve it. By ego, I mean our desire to be always right and thinking that we are. Then work together towards achieving this goal of learning, and we have creativity. These types of creative movements do not occur very often, have a specific location and are dependent on finding a very inspirational goal.

But what if we could reverse engineer these creative movements, so that we learned how to harness the ego? Not by distracting the ego with an inspirational goal, but through reasoning. What if we could simply explain what the ego is and discover and explain the method used to harness it? Rethink Perfect is my proposal to harness the ego, reduce the possibility of conflict and aggression, and possibly encourage diverse and creative thinking. Like creativity, conflict starts with a spark, but instead of fanning its flames, we need to extinguish the spark of conflict as soon as possible. In Ken Robinson's book "Out of Our Minds - Learning to be Creative" he says:

"Creativity flourishes when there is a systematic strategy to promote it. The cultural environment should be modeled on the dynamics of intelligence. Many organisations stifle creativity in the structures they inhabit and the ethos they promote. If the ideas are discouraged or ignored, the creative impulse does one of two things. It deserts or subverts the organisation."

Basically, what I am saying is that the sharing of diverse and dissenting views can be one of the best tools for assisting the creative process. Having agreed rules of engagement in place "a systematic strategy", to define how we converse can lead to more productive conversing and innovation. It is no coincidence that these creative movements were location based which leads me to believe they were founded on prolific sharing of ideas face to face. Just imagine how many conversations must have taken place to influence each participant in these movements or projects. Without these conversations, would such creative periods in our history ever have existed? Somehow, I doubt it. Now imagine we had an improved method of conversing that facilitated the converting of concepts more and subverting of relationships less. Conversing on steroids! Well, I guess I am hoping that someday Rethink Perfect will be able to do just that.

Conversation, Creativity and Converting Our Concepts: In Alan Rowe's book *Creative Intelligence*, he states: "A quantum leap is needed to deal with changing external forces", and goes on to say that "Leaders who are concerned with significant change need to *convince* their organisations to accept new ideas". Now some or most of you will probably agree with this, but I don't. What I am about to propose, I think, is potentially a quantum leap that can nurture the creative intelligence that he mentions.

I don't think that we need to "convince" our organisations, nor convert anyone in them. I think we need to convert our own concepts only, through the feedback from the people in these organisations. This is not the same thing. I think this is the paradigm shift in how we converse with each other. Understanding that the conversation is composed of converse ideas where we are conversely speaking. We are not in agreement. We are using the conversation to form agreements. But by converting our own concepts and not others' during conversation, we can approach the conversation with a completely different attitude. If we are trying to convince others, we spend more time trying to convert their ideas and not our own. It is a very static, dogmatic and egoistic approach that is similar to the title of Edward de Bono's book, *I Am Right You Are Wrong*. However, de Bono had his tongue firmly placed in his cheek when choosing this title. The best thing about Rethink Perfect is that we can even use the views of people that are trying to convert us, as long as we can *Appreciate* their contribution. Then we apply the last 3 As of the 6A framework and ask them to explain their views in ways that will encourage us to help them. eg. By at least supplying their reasoning and or experience.

Rowe goes on to say, "Using the right words is especially important when trying to convince employees to accept personal risk. This is more easily said than done." I agree with you, Alan. I think making the shift from "converting or convincing others" to "converting or convincing ourselves" is the quantum leap in our vocabulary that is needed for the twenty first century.

The Right Words Needed: Even in the recently published book *Enchantment*: *The Art of Changing Hearts, Minds, and Actions* by Guy Kawasaki, his title gives away what I call the old twentieth century way of thinking. A good read, but still his goal is to change the hearts, minds and actions of others. Guy references the old classic by Dale Carnegie, *How to Win Friends and Influence People* (1934), which also falls into this category of what I call "old school thinking". What I am advocating is the next step in our development that we achieve by asking ourselves, "What can I say and do to get others to help me change my concepts and ideas?" My version of

Kawasaki's book would be called; *The Art of Using Conversation to Change My Own Heart, Mind and Actions*, and it would show how to use others' diverse ideas to stimulate one's own changing or creativity.

I'm the only person I know, other than my brother, who has this idea about conversation and conversions, and we certainly could be wrong - I am open to any feedback (but don't forget your reasoning). I only have one agreement on this concept so far, and it is yet to be fully tested, especially within interpersonal relationships. So I am not trying to convince anyone here. What I am saying is if anyone can help me convert my concept further, I would be truly grateful to receive your diverse feedback or dissent.

Your Feedback is Much Appreciated: By this stage, you probably liked some of the things I have mentioned and disliked other parts. For some, much of it probably sounded Greek to you. Great! Please feel free to send me an email or use the feedback box on my blog to share your thoughts and questions. After all, I am writing this to convert my concepts, not to try converting you, right? I can also give you feedback on your concepts to help you convert them into possible agreements and new solutions for us both. This is, and will probably always be, a work in progress. The main idea of this chapter is that conversation can be so much more than what we have thought in the past. It was through conversations that the USA was able to put a man on the moon. The country plotted a goal, having possibly millions of conversations that helped them convert their concepts, and made their idea a reality 10 years later.

Your feedback is very much appreciated and always worth considering: So how will I know if someone is trying to convert me rather than trying to convert their own ideas from my feedback? I guess it doesn't really matter, as it might well be that any feedback is worth considering - either to help correct my concept or shore up my argument that old thinking tries to convert others, and new thinking tries to convert our own thinking. Let's see which one you have or if you disagree with this concept, and why.

Priming: If someone is really seeking feedback, they will tell me what they are doing and why. When someone is seeking to convert me, they will tell me what I should be doing and how to do it. Or they will use emotionally-charged language that is not adjustable or accountable, and therefore is unacceptable to me. This type of expression is designed to prime me into acquiescing to their view. However, if someone feels like it is necessary to try to convert me, it might possibly be because they feel that I am trying to convert them. By using Appreciation, Acknowledging and Apology, I can relieve this. If we agreed to use the Dispute Moderator, we could simply refer to it if we felt lost. I suppose that if I continue to remind them and myself that I do not want to convert them, but rather get their feedback to convert my concepts, it should help me relieve their fear and allow them to simply give me feedback on what I am doing, and vice versa.

Feedback Loops: It is no wonder that the art of conversation is lost, since "feedback" comprises such an important other half of conversation.

How can we disagree with feedback? Of course logically, we can't disagree with its content as it is only someone else's reflection on our thought or action. What we can disagree with is the delivery. This is basically the premise that the concept of Rethink Perfect rests on. That if we could agree upon this and had the tools to help filter the feedback delivery from the content, we could possibly find ourselves listening to well-delivered feedback that could represent the pure thought of another person. This could change life as we know it.

"Does my bum look big in this?" is the joke that everyone in a relationship can identify with, especially us blokes. Most men, I believe, live in perpetual fear of saying the "wrong" thing.

The question is kind of a trap. You see she didn't ask him what he thinks, which would have been an easier question to answer. She asked him a general question or what the world would think of her bum. By answering "yes" at that point, he is going to be in trouble because his feedback delivery is flawed. I bet you agree with me on his fate. But real issues arise because he can get in "trouble" in the first place. He is not a six-year-old boy that stole sixpence. He contributed his flawed feedback. This should first and foremost be appreciated.

So, what is it that made his delivery flawed? Well, as mentioned, I do not believe that we can disagree with the content of his remark as it is only his opinion. His delivery was flawed because he did not emphasise that he was expressing his opinion, i.e., "I think it does look big" or "to me it looks big". (I can't help but snigger as I write this). Even if he had answered "no" it would still have been flawed feedback in the delivery, and he would possibly suffer for this answer too, sometime later.

I think that if we can learn to understand this principle of splitting up feedback into content and delivery, and not disagree or agree with the content but only return our feedback on their delivery, some very interesting results could be achieved in conversation. The conversing treasure, that has been lost for so long, could return along with the gems of creative ideas that "real" and diverse conversation can form.

"The truce will set you free"

Chapter 7 Direct Feedback Moment - DFM

Truce in Conversation or Agreed Method of Disengagement: The goal of this chapter is to create and agree to use a tool that will pause a conversation when one of us thinks we have reached a point where we cannot achieve an agreement with the available information. This is what I call a truce. Nevertheless, during the pause, we would still be engaged in our own thought process, trying to resolve the conversation/dispute or disagreement. The challenge was to come up with a tool that would replace such idioms as: "If you can't stand the heat, *get out* of the *kitchen*", *"Let's agree to disagree"* or *"let it go"*. A DFM or Direct Feedback Moment is just the tool to take the heat out of a dispute. It is the conscious activation of Rethink Perfect, especially when one of us feels that we are in danger of losing control of the conversation. DFM is a plan to deal with such a situation. I have created my own idioms that go more like *"Let's agree how to disagree"* or *"Let's disagree to agree"*. *(Which confuses everyone, even me).*

Truce −noun

1. A suspension of hostilities for a specified period of time by mutual agreement of the warring parties; cease-fire; armistice.

2. An agreement or treaty establishing this.

3. A temporary respite, as from trouble or pain.

58

Even in war, it is understood that there are agreed protocols to suspend hostilities. I don't believe we have something similar for conversations or discussions that have reached a dispute or disagreement and are possibly heading for an argument or a conflict of sorts. A DFM is like a spare parachute or an airbag, more to be used in case of emergencies.

Feedback is a Mirror or Reflection: As I mentioned in the previous chapter, your feedback is always worth considering, especially if I don't like it. I don't think it is possible for me to disagree with it, as it is only feedback on what I have said or done. It is a bit like looking in the mirror and not liking what I see. Feedback is a reflection of sorts on what I have said or done. Not liking it is one thing, smashing the mirror is another. If I don't like what I see, I can try to change my message or change myself and lose some weight. But blaming the mirror for what it reflects is an act of madness, I think.

That reminds me of a story: A man reported on his Facebook page that when he looked in the mirror, he noticed he had lost nearly 20 kilos. Someone wrote to him asking where they could buy that mirror!

How Does a DFM Work?: A DFM is the place and time that we have planned for when we reach a point where either person wants to disengage from the discussion. It allows us to "bookmark" where we are in the discussion so that we can resume and resolve our conversation/dispute at a later time after doing some further research or rethinking. Once agreed to, it is a tool that we use to open and close controversial issues in a prescribed way. For example, "I think....." to open, and "Your feedback is worth considering" to close. Failure to use a DFM in an agreed manner can result in conflict and failure in the conversation.

Some rules of engagement for a DFM:
(These rules are rough and need to be refined)

- A DFM is called by the person that offered the initial feedback. Ie "Can I give you a DFM..."
- The person seeking the initial feedback can suggest the other to give them a DFM if they are being too indirect.
- It works best in a one-on-one environment
- It can be modified and enhanced to make it easier to accept by the recipient.

Feedback Loops Making Us Loopy: So let me try running this past you. A teacher or parent shares with their student or child what they have learned throughout their experience in life to date.

What the student or child shares back is their feedback on this information from their point of view.

If the teacher or parent then marks or evaluates the content of the student or child's feedback, a couple of things could happen:

1. It will inhibit the student or child from disagreeing openly with the teacher or parent because the child or student is well aware of the feedback loop and that it is a no win situation.

2. You start to get a feedback loop and not a good result for either side.

So what is the solution? All the teacher or parent can do is evaluate the delivery process that the student or child employed to give their feedback on the shared knowledge. For example, if the student said, "That's crap!" The teacher could reply, "Thanks, Jane, for your feedback. However, a couple of pointers on your delivery: 1. Are you saying that you think it is crap, or that it conforms to a universal description of crap? 2. I am sorry that I did not get a prior agreement with you regarding how to

60

give feedback, but I would like us to agree that we use the 3 A's of: thanks for letting me know.....(Appreciate), sorry that I don't agree...(Apologise), but I think such-and-such about your point....(Acknowledge). 3. That I cannot very well give you feedback on your feedback of my point or we will simply enter into a feedback loop at this point. So if you did use the 3A's and told me why you thought it was crap, I would be better off considering and appreciating it for another time and place when I have fully absorbed it and your reasoning, and avoid any feedback loops."

This type of thinking regarding Feedback Loops could actually give us a number of things that I have been looking for:

This could be the "Truce in a Conversation" or the "Agreement Point".

Awareness of this loop could stop the discussion/ conversation from ever getting so hot that we need a tool to "get out of the kitchen". Arguments and fights might just be the result of these "feedback loops", where no one is stopping for a moment to reflect upon what was said. Instead, both go loopy!

Chapter 8 My Relationship Treaty

Golden Rule: It is probably a coincidence that my last name is Sherlock, but this has turned out to be one very long investigation that has lasted 26 years to date. I sometimes think if only we had a built-in Black Box Recorder, like those found on all commercial planes, and also had the mandate to investigate every failed relationship, then maybe we could reduce the high marital failure rate that exists in the western world today. Well, maybe we do have a built-in "Black Box" that is called "experience", and maybe we were all offered the mandate to investigate using our desire in the context of following the Golden Rule by treating others as we *desire* to have others treat us.

I think that the more we can explain and define how we *desire* to be treated, the more we can consciously treat others according to the same standards. This is nothing new; it is just putting into action what is required from the Golden Rule. How can we treat others as we want to be treated if we don't exactly know how we want to be treated? As you can see, finding this out could be a lifelong process and has been the catalyst for this book. The general pattern now seems to be that we get to "know" each other first, and later learn how we like to be treated. As we learn how we would like to be treated and realise that our partner is not capable (which can take years), we then complain about them and the whole process. I propose that we learn how we prefer to be treated *first* and share those preferences upfront. If anything, it could save us a lot of time and heartache. Who knows, I may have rediscovered an ancient way to find our soul mate. If you set out to discover this information on your own, you could end up like me, reaching the age of 50 before being able to explain your desires. Or you may want to profit vicariously by learning from my efforts here, and save yourself a heap of time and energy.

Time to Treat Myself: "I will treat others the way I would like to be treated" is known as the Golden Rule or the Law of Reciprocity, as per Hugh MacKay's comment in *What Makes us Tick*. I call it the Golden Treaty, since it is all about how we *treat* each other. But as simple as it sounds, it seems like the devil is in the detail. For example, ask me to simply answer how I would like to be treated and I might say, "Give me lots of money, chocolate cake, rub my feet and scratch my back when requested." So, does that mean that I should treat others in the same way? Well, maybe. This is obviously going to take some time to work out. It is almost like we have been granted three wishes, and we need to come up with the very best of wishes that will have the most important impact on our own and also other people's lives. Rethink Perfect and its 6 rules of engagement is about determining how I would like to be treated and getting these agreed to, in principle, upfront. It represents what I call "my relationship treaty" or the consideration that I am seeking from my mate – a kind of guide as to how we would treat each other in our relationship. If I were a penguin, it would be my reply to her squawk and peck that she sends in my direction during our mating cycle or courtship, hoping for correspondence.

How I got to this Point: It would be remiss of me to continue if I did not mention how I got to this point in my thinking. My heartfelt thanks go out to my "ex". Not so much my ex-wife, but my ex-perimental relationship. It was some 12 years ago, in August 1998, that I agreed to help a young woman stay in Australia, if she would help me test all my theories on love and relationships. What a deal, I thought. How could I resist, considering that I had been working on my concepts for some 13 years at that point and had never had a chance to test them in a relationship? So I accepted her offer and we spent the next 2 years testing my ideas/concepts. Well, I have to be honest: they failed me miserably. I had to rethink them all and basically start from scratch. In August 2000, 2 years to the day after we began our experiment, we parted company. Kate achieved Australian residency and I got my incredible experiment, which included so many experiences that I could have written a book on this alone. One year after we split Kate returned to Siberia never to return to Australia but we still keep in touch occasionally. *I wish to emphasise that I did not bring her to Australia. That although it was an experimental relationship we had a fairly standard living arrangement, for a standard marriage. Which included a miscarriage and possibly a fair bit more disputing going on than a standard relationship.

One thing of note and in context to this book is how we got married, which was within a few weeks of meeting. After the celebrate asked if we would take each other as husband and wife, we both replied "I'll try". Later, after the impromptu ceremony in his shop front, and with the witnesses from next door, I asked him how many couples he had married. He replied, "About 500". I then asked him how many had said I'll try and he replied that we were the first two.

Probably the most important thing that I learned from my experience was when I asked Kate, out of desperation one night, how I should act when she was complaining to me irresponsibly (what I considered nagging), she replied that I could simply say, "Thanks for letting me know that you have a problem, but now can you talk to me in a way that is going to encourage me to help you". As soon as I heard this, I knew I had found something special. But it is only now, some 11 years later, that I truly appreciate what she taught me.

So I guess I have learned two valuable lessons:

1. That the value of conversing is not necessarily apparent at the time, but may be revealed much later. In my case, some

conversations have instructed me as long as 40 years later. Wow!

2. That feedback can be split into two parts during the conversation: into content. i.e. "Thanks for letting me know" and into delivery, i.e., "Can you talk to me in a way that will encourage me to help you". It is only now that I am really starting to see the value of this in the context of conversing and feedback, and how it is a vital part of this whole concept of Rethink Perfect.

So I can truly thank Kate from the bottom of my heart for two of the most valuable and trying years of my life. Although I would not like to have to relive that time with nothing but the tools that I had then, I do believe that I am just about ready to try a new relationship with my latest ideas that form this book, Rethink Perfect.

The Social Trend Verses Diversity: In 1988, when I was 28, I wrote this poem in New Zealand in my quest to understand the mating cycle:

The Penguin
The penguin male sits upon the shore
The mating cycle begins in earnest.
She arrives in early spring,
to make her yearly conquest

A call, a squawk, a thrust of their beak,
This drive within to correspond.
To find the perfect partner,
or renew an everlasting bond.

Unceasingly these winds unwind
as male and female weld.
Instinct is the perfect way,
the social trend upheld.

But what of man and womanhood
As their beastly ways unfold?
Instinct is the perfect way
and this should we uphold?

What and where is the social trend?
And does the greatest number rule?
What squawk and thrust should I make?
Has instinct become the fool?

A "treaty" is defined as:

1. A formal agreement between two or more states in reference to peace, alliance, commerce, or other international relations.

2. Any agreement or compact.

I guess the closest thing to a relationship treaty today is the vows that are said and signed for in a marriage or matrimonial ceremony. I have been working on my pact, accord, or treaty for some 26 years and hopefully I am pretty close to signing off (metaphorically) on it. It's turning out that I am considering a treaty without a pact, an agreement without a signed document, or what is known as a non-binding agreement - what I call a Rethink Agreement.

Some people might scoff at my efforts, but I say if airliners crashed as often as relationships do at present, then I doubt if anyone would risk air travel. Rethink Perfect is about realising that something that breaks on average around 50% of the time is far from perfect and needs some serious overhauling. If people chose their so-called life partners more carefully, as though it were a life or death decision, then I think more people would put more effort into finding their own relationship treaty, or use an existing one such as Rethink Perfect.

Rethink Perfect is my relationship treaty that I propose to use with my partner to peacefully co-exist; first, as a way to moderate any disputes with each other, and then to move forward and build a prosperous life and family together. It is my treaty or "squawk and peck" that I have chosen to find my mate or more so, help her to find me.

I also think that this form of treaty is transferable to other relationships in my life, such as with any offspring she might have with me in the future or with my siblings and parents. It may even be possible that it can be used in my business partnerships and with my boss or employees. At this point, however, all of this is an art not a science and this treaty needs to be tested, proved/disproved and converted into better understood agreements.

I consider Rethink Perfect to be the essence of quality equality. As a work in progress, it is how I would like to be treated and how I would be willing to reciprocate with someone. It is the culmination of over 50 A5 journals filled with my thoughts on relationships, my experimental relationship and of countless conversations with people, about what they think makes relationships tick or crack.

Rethink Perfect is about being willing to look again or reconsider any thought on relationships at any time, with nothing being solid or allowed to form a dogma. No one being above reproach and every concept open to be questioned and allowed to stand to agreed reasoning.

Rethink Perfect serves as my mating cycle, my mating cry, which will hopefully repel the ones that are not suited to me and attract the ones that may be, out of the vast array of choice that we all have in this globalised world that we now live in. Below is the beginning of a conversation that I think we need to have. Within the context of Rethink Perfect and the 6As tentatively agreed to, I would like to enter into such a conversation and who knows what results we will uncover.

Who Should Initiate?: One question that has had me stumped for years is who should initiate with whom? That is, should the man take the initiative or the woman? Now, when I ask this question, most people tell me that either one can and does initiate, and that it is equally done nowadays. At least they admit that in the past, it has been expected that the guy will make the first move.

So now it is apparently equal. Well, even if this were the case, I believe that it is incumbent upon the woman to initiate or at least take a more proactive role in selecting and I will explain why.

I am talking about the *mating cycle* here. Couples get together with the long-term goal of eventually producing a family. In this situation, I think it would be far better for a woman to initiate than a man since, in this situation, they are forming a partnership to have a child or children. She physically has the children, and he is the assistant child producer. She takes nine months to produce the baby, and he spends about nine minutes and any assistance that he contributes during the pregnancy.

It is her baby, for all intents and purposes. She has the right to abort if she so chooses, even if he does not agree. If they split up within the first few years, it is she that would get the bulk custody of the child. She does by far the most amount of work during the pregnancy and so rightfully deserves this recognition. No one could argue with this, I don't think. So she is responsible for production and he is the assistant. Wouldn't it make sense, then, that she would advertise for her "assistant's" position to be filled? And that she interview the candidates to make sure that *he* is going to be suited for this very important position?

So she advertises and he responds. How does this play out in the mating cycle? I am not sure, but I do not believe that guys going up to as many women as they can and playing the numbers game is going to achieve the appropriate result for such a mating cycle and could explain why a lot of relationships end up breaking. I think that when a man initiates it is only for one reason: sex for pleasure. It can't be sex for producing his offspring as they are not *his* they are hers. When a woman initiates, it could be for one of maybe three or four reasons: sex for pleasure, sex for producing *her* offspring, sex for both of those reasons or sex for money. This will always keep a man on his toes, as he would never really know her end goal at the time. When a man initiates, it should be pretty obvious what his end goal is. He may not even realise this, but believe me, men cannot have a child. (Well not when this book was written).

Understanding this, I have been reluctant to initiate and have waited patiently over the past 25 years for a woman that understands what I consider to be her part in the mating cycle. Most people have scoffed at this, predicting that I would be waiting a long time. They have been right so far, but at least my concept has kept me out of trouble to date. And somehow I find it difficult to believe that just because the majority may believe in something different to me, does not make them more "right", by virtue of numbers. It could very well be the blind leading the blind.

The Cost of Sexual Relations: I think that if everyone had the conversation about the true costs of having sex, that we would all be a lot more cautious about choosing our sex partners. So what are the costs? Well as Clair Weaver reports in her article "The Problem with Marriage and Relationships", Sunday Telegraph January 13, 2008:

"It is estimated that in Australia some $100 million per month is lost in settlements due to the failure of marriages or cohabitation relationships. In the US, it is estimated that this figure is around $1.5 - 2 billion per month, and worldwide the figure is upwards of a staggering $10 - 15 billion per month. This constitutes the world's largest ongoing financial and social catastrophe."

These figures are the financial costs borne chiefly by the men in divorce settlements. Untallied are the social costs to women that have to bear the main burden of bringing up their children after the divorce. But most importantly, the emotional costs borne by her children in dealing with such breakups are not included. Imagine if all of the social costs of a breakup were fully discussed before a relationship even began. That is, before we had sex. Maybe this is one way to curb such catastrophic social and financial costs associated with matrimonial breakups.

There is one way, however that I think us males can have our *own* offspring or progeny, or at least become a more equal contributor and bear a lot more responsibility for child birth. That is, to hang around and contribute financially, intellectually and emotionally to the child's upbringing. Now of course this happens today but maybe it is occurring for the wrong reasoning. That is, out of obligation and commitment rather than understanding or "love". But imagine if we both agreed that I would contribute for at least nine years. That is, one year for every month she spends pregnant. After this time the relationship could be renegotiated and we both could decide if we still wanted to remain in the relationship. That it takes some nine years for the family to adopt me, as the father, into it, if I pulled my weight.

If this was valid reasoning of the mating cycle, then it would give me a "real" reason to be supportive. Saving her from having to create "unreasonable certainty", trying to get me to acquiesce and promise in the name of "commitment" and ultimately compromise myself. All done under the banner of so-called "love" and "matrimony".

Matri – *mother,* mony – *state of, or condition*
"The Mother Condition".

As reasonable as this sounds to me, it is obviously quite a radical proposal and I am sure that some of you will want to disagree with my reasoning. Great! But maybe the time has come to rethink a tradition that has been considered perfect and therefore neglected for far too long. With the poor state that matrimony is in today, maybe a few radical ideas need to be put out there and with the help of Rethink Perfect and its rules of engagement, the real conversation can begin. So please contribute to the discussion, by going to my website Rethinkperfect.com and add your descent or endorsement.

Chapter 9 Biron's Quest, a Fairy Tale

About Biron: Biron was written in 1988 when I was 28 and searching for answers that I didn't even have the questions for. Now in 2012, some 24 years later, I have also developed the answers and questions that help explain what the flying and wings metaphors mean to me.

Biron Outline: Biron is a young bird in a flock of birds that has lost the ability to fly. This is a story of how he saw that there was something missing in his life and how he went about rectifying it. With Rethink Perfect in mind, it is a chance to see how Biron was searching for feedback to convert his very basic concept on what his wings were for and how he eventually found a new solution to a problem that only he believed existed.

Biron's Quest, a Fairy Tale

Nestled at the base of a huge red rock lay a deep red, desert plain, sparsely decorated with clumps of dry grass, gums and trees. Some small water holes were dotted around the rock, otherwise the setting was vast and dry, with only the screeching of birds giving any indication of life. This land was peculiar, however, as there was not a bird to be seen in the sky or perched in any of the trees. All built their nests upon the ground amongst the grass tufts, and they walked on the red sand to their not too distant destinations. This is the story of Biron, just one of many young birds who lived contented in his parents' nest, until one fateful morning. A layer of mist settled on the plain as the distant sun broke the horizon and glistened on their frost encrusted nests and the surrounding grasses.

73

Biron was playing nearby when out of the blue a question popped into his head that he had never heard before and had no answer for, so he decided to ask his mother.

"Mum, what are our wings for?" he asked innocently, expecting her to satisfy his curiosity immediately. Biron was not quite prepared for his mother's reaction: she suddenly stopped doing her morning chores and seemed agitated. Impatient, he began to repeat his inquiry.

"Mauuum ......"!

"Biron, what a silly question", she swiftly interjected. "We all know what our wings are for and that is that. I didn't have to ask my parents such a question, and I don't think you should be worrying us or yourself about such trivial matters."

In an instant, Biron's peaceful existence was shattered. He was not satisfied with his mother's reply, and he wondered why she was so agitated.

Deciding not to pursue the matter any further at this point, he headed towards the creek where he knew he would find his father. Biron knew that his mother had a short temper and he was not about to get his tail feather plucked just because he wanted an unclouded answer. Perhaps his father would be more cooperative, he thought. Biron arrived at a place where a channel separated from the creek to form a large billabong. This was where most of the older male birds gathered. Each one squawked and pecked as though they had something very important to say. It didn't take Biron very long to find his father, as he had a favorite drinking spot. Biron asked his dad what he thought his wings were for.

"Biron, go on back to the nest", he scorned, "and don't you be bothering your mother with such foolish questions."

This time, Biron was not so surprised by his father's reaction, but was still despondent and confused. Swiftly, he retreated from the watering hole, and then sluggishly returned to the nest. With head down and mind deep in thought, he wondered how such a simple question could cause his parents to get into such a flap.

His mind began to run in search of an answer and he still wished to know what his wings were really for. Thus began Biron's quest.

II

It was a few days later, while taking a leisurely stroll around the billabong and basking in the mid-day sun, that Biron saw two lovebirds fawning over each other. "Yuck!!" thought Biron. They came closer with a glazed look in their eyes, confirming their dazed emotional state. Out of desperation, he distracted them from their preoccupation long enough to inquire what they thought wings were for.

"Wings were for shade, eh... to keep the sun off our bodies during the summer!" one answered, as though she had stated the obvious.

"And to keep us warm in the cold winter months" the other reiterated, looking to her for confirmation, as a child would to an adult. "Really, though, it is up to the individual as to what we think wings are for", she replied.

"Birds are not all the same", her mate said, backing her up.

"If they were, the world sure would be a boring place to live", she concluded, chuckling falsely.

He smiled knowingly, and they completed their responses by nodding their heads as though they had counterbalances attached. Biron knew of these uses but he wanted to know if wings had a specialised use, one that was indisputably correct.

He believed that both the birds favored the answer that they had given. By concluding that it was up to the individual to decide, they could avoid their differences. Testing his theory, he asked them for the reasons for what they thought. Suddenly, the conversation became cold and unfriendly. Biron was accused of hijacking the discussion by interrogating them.

"What is the problem?" Biron pleaded innocently. "It's your attitude", she replied. "You are just not listening to us", said the other. "We already told you our opinion and we don't think that we can add any more." "You are entitled to believe what you believe, but don't try to force it down our throats." They ended their conversation then and there, walking off quickly, talking between themselves, turning back to look at Biron now and then until he was finally out of view. "Birds of a feather", thought Biron.

Poor Biron, he felt so sad. He did not even have the chance to ask the birds why they thought his parents had been so angry. He guessed that it may have been the same reason that they had been. 'What was wrong with my attitude?' he wondered. "Should I just agree or keep silent, even if I do not understand, or believe them to be correct?"

Biron talked to many birds along the plain, asking them about their wings, and about the attitude his parents had to the question. Each time the conversation began pleasantly, but when he asked for their reasons, the same aggressive standoff resulted as had occurred with his parents and the two lovebirds. He heard many answers to his first question, 'To keep the rain off our heads', 'For keeping our balance when running' and 'To keep our heads covered while we are sleeping'. Each bird believing their use to be the most important one, but usually completed their answers by saying that it was up to the individual to decide, and that more than one answer was correct.

Biron was still confused. Instead of getting answers, he was gathering more questions. After each conversation, he would be told in various ways to stop looking for a problem that did not exist. He was told that their reasons were private or personal. Biron wanted to know why they thought it was private and how could it be a personal issue, as all birds had wings. He was also told to have more respect and to accept what other birds had to say. Yet he did not think that he was rejecting their answers, he just wanted to know their reasons for them. 'How can I accept an idea that I did not fully understand or agree with?' he thought, and 'How can I respect a bird that expected me to accept an untested idea?' Biron suspected that they did not have any reasons of their own, and were trying to hide that fact. He did not know why, but he was just as determined to find out the answer to this question, just as he wanted to uncover what his wings were really for.

On one occasion, when Biron was strolling along the stream, he met a wise old, grey-feathered bird. She was tolerant and patient, allowing Biron to ask all his questions and to explain the trouble he seemed to be causing.

"I was once like you and asked myself the same question", she said. "But I never had the courage to ask any other bird. You see, I was worried what the other birds would say. After all, it was not the type of question a bird would normally ask. It has been accepted by the flock that wings have particular uses, and that is that. Why should a bird question it further, especially if it is going to cause such conflict? Besides, there are so many other issues to be considered in life before wings."

"Have you ever thought of a use for wings that no other bird talks about?" Biron asked enthusiastically.

"No. But I do remember, when I was a little critter like yourself, my grand pappi telling me something about a thing called 'flying'. He had heard about it from his grand pappi, but he did not know exactly what it was, only that it was something to do with wings."

Biron rubbed his bottom beak and wondered what this "flying" could be. He had never heard of it before and wondered if any other bird had. This would be his next question. He thanked the wise, old, grey-feathered bird and departed with a renewed confidence. Biron felt that he had stumbled upon a gold nugget and he was not about to throw it away now. He thought that all the abuse that he had received was worth it, just for the chance to talk to the wise old bird and hear about this flying thing. By this stage, word had got around that Biron was asking weird questions. The birds in the flock did not like any other bird to be overly different from themselves. Biron was certainly acting as though he was. Some of the birds that Biron had spoken to did think that his questions were interesting, but like the grey-feathered bird, did not have the courage to ask any other bird. They did not believe the risk or effort to be worth it, thinking the question would never be answered. Biron was not convinced.

As he continued asking his questions, he began to realise that no bird had any substantial reasoning for what they thought, and none cared enough to find out. He believed that they were all afraid of each other. If the fear is this big, he thought, then maybe the answer is just as big. A thrill shot through his little body. He felt like an intrepid explorer trying to uncover a long lost city. He might become an outcast because of his inquiry, but his hope of finding an answer was increasing with each encounter. This gave him the desire to continue.

III

A few weeks later, while Biron was taking a stroll around the vast red rock, he heard a distant rumbling. It slowly became louder until he thought he was going to die. Biron looked up in despair, a saw a shiny silver object quite a distance in the air and directly above him. He had never seen such a thing before and was absolutely terrified. Biron lay on the ground with his wing covering his eyes until the object seemed to pass and the noise diminished. Finally, he got back to his feet just in time to see the object sail off into the distance. "Whew!" he exclaimed in relief. He stood staring at this object that had scared him so. Immediately his inquisitive mind began to ask, 'What was it?' 'How did it get up so high in the sky?' and 'Why did it not fall to the ground?' His first thought was that it looked like a stiff worm with outstretched wings in the middle and rear. He looked down at his wings as he compulsively tried to extend them. He quickly restored them to their normal position, since he had neither the strength nor the agility to hold them out for long. Biron wondered if this was the real use for wings. Perhaps this was the 'flying' that the grey-feathered bird had spoken of. He raced back to the valley, to his parents' nest. "Mum!" he cried, trying to catch his breath and slow down as he approached her.

"Mum, did you see that thing as it went across the sky?", he asked excitedly. "Yes", she replied casually. Biron stepped lightly. "Mum, do you know what 'flying' is?" "Ah yes", she answered in a pleasant tone. Biron thought that finally he was getting somewhere. "Flying was something that my mother told me about when I was a little chick no older than yourself. It is a very personal feeling that is very difficult to explain". Biron was waiting impatiently. "But what is it used for?" "Well, it is not exactly used for any one thing in particular. It is more of a feeling one gets. Now don't ask me any more questions, you will just have to experience it for yourself some day." "What do you mean by personal?" Biron asked knowing that he was pushing it. "Look, you will just know when you are flying. Now, don't ask me any more questions".

Biron was not impressed. None of that made any sense to him. How would he know when he was 'flying' if he did not know what flying was? And why had his mother not mentioned this 'flying' before now? He would have liked to continue his conversation with his mother, but he was afraid of the consequences. He began to ask other birds what they thought 'flying' might be. He also asked them about the object in the sky and if they thought that it had anything to do with 'flying'. Most agreed with his mother, saying the topic was not worth pursuing. Some got aggressive, refusing to continue the conversation, reminding him once again of his attitude problem.

Biron concluded that his theory was worth putting to the test. He began to lift his wings as high and for as long as he could, believing that if he practiced enough he would get the strength to hold his wings out for a sufficient time to 'fly'. Every day he practiced - up, down, up, down. His mother did not know what he was trying to do. Biron tried to explain, but she could not understand what lifting his wings had to do with flying.

"Biron, I told you what flying was and you just haven't listened", she scorned.

He continued to practice as often as he could, determined to prove a point as much as he was to fly. He knew that if he failed that he would look a fool. He was prepared to take the risk. Up, down, up, down. All the other birds also wondered what he was trying to achieve. They laughed and jeered at the bird that asked so many unusual questions, and now performed such absurd movements. For weeks he practiced. By now he could hold his wings out long enough to notice a feeling of lightness as the wind blew into his face. He knew then that he was onto something that was more than just a 'feeling'.

He continued to exercise week after week. His strength continued to increase until one day it happened quite unexpectedly.

While Biron was exercising up in the hills, a gust of wind lifted him up into the air. Biron was in a state of shock as he soared twelve metres. Suddenly, more out of fear than lack of control, he tilted to the left and plummeted back to earth. What a mess. Biron's feathers were all ruffled, and some were scattered on the ground where he had crashed. He lay under a bush a few metres from the place of impact, his eyes closed, the wind knocked out of him. He did not know if he was badly hurt, but he knew that he had been flying, which helped him forget about his aches and pains.

After a few moments, he was able to get back to his feet. He cautiously brushed his feathers back into place and checked for any major damage. None. He was still in a daze as he swayed down the hill, both from the crash and from the experience of having flown. He told his mother about his encounter with the wind and the ground, but she did not take much interest. No bird seemed to believe or pay any attention to him. They laughed when Biron told them how he had fallen out of the sky, assuring him that even if he did "fly" that it was far too dangerous, as his crash had shown. Biron found it hard to understand their negative attitude. He cautiously resumed his practice, deciding to allow the wind to lift him only a metre or so above the ground. He thought that it would be much safer until he became more skilful. For hours he flapped and glided in the wind.

Finally, more than a week after his first flight and disaster, he allowed the wind to lift him into the sky.

It was a moment that he would never forget for the rest of his life, and would never want to. With just a slight breeze blowing in his face, he took a couple of extended flaps and began a controlled ascent. Taking a deep breath for every flap, he extended his wings even further. Gracefully he rose, until he felt that he was high enough to turn.

He pictured in his mind how he was going to maneuver - it was as though he had always known how. Raising his head and chest, he slowed and then stalled. At the same time Biron dropped his left wing and began to fall to the left. He quickly picked up speed, spread his wings and was soon sailing away with the wind, floating high above the desert plain.

After a few more maneuvers, he began to notice the scenery around him and was elated. There were no words that could have expressed how Biron was feeling at that moment. All of his questions had been answered in an instant, all of his efforts had been justified, and his direction in the future had been specified. Around and around he went, soaring higher and higher, bathing himself in his accomplishment.

Eventually, Biron came back to earth both emotionally and physically, coming to rest on the branch of a tree that overlooked the valley. He thought about his parents and the rest of the birds, believing that they would finally listen to him when they saw him flying. He gathered his breath while he pondered. His fitness needed to improve considerably. Within a short time he had recovered enough to resume flying and decided to fly home and show his mother what he had achieved.

He took to the air, this time with very little thought as though he had been flying all of his life. When he arrived over his parents' nest, he circled a few times, hoping that his mother would see him. "Mum!" he cried. "Look at me!" She looked all around her, not knowing where Biron's voice had come from.

"Mu-uuum!!" he shrieked. This time she looked up to see Biron gliding towards her. She ducked and covered her head with her wing, thinking that he was going to hit her. "Hi, mum", Biron said casually, as though he had just walked in.

"Biron, what were you doing up there?" she barked. "You could have hurt yourself."

Biron said nothing. He wanted to see if she had noticed that he had actually been flying. But she also said nothing, and they stood there in silence. His mother was too proud to

82

acknowledge that her son had found something that was new and exciting - something that she had not known existed. Finally Biron spoke.

"Well, what do you think"? Biron's mum stated in a worried tone. "What will the neighbors think?"

"Don't worry about them mum, this is flying, this is what our wings were really made for".

"Are you sure? It does not look very safe to me".

"Yes, I am sure. With a bit of practice, you will be doing somersaults".

"No, I still think that flying is something else", she replied. "And I certainly don't think that I will be travelling through the air like that."

"But mum ..." "No. I know what flying is and that is that! Now don't start your questions again. I don't think that I can take any more".

Biron was dumbfounded.

He could not understand why his mother was acting that way. He thought that he would fly down to the big trees near the stream and surprise his dad. Maybe he would share Biron's excitement. He took to the air with his hopes slightly dented by his mother's indifference. Fortunately, the exhilaration he experienced from flying quickly renewed them.

He flew around the billabong a few times, hoping to spot his father amongst the other birds. "Hello down there", Biron yelled enthusiastically. The birds looked up momentarily, then continued their conversations as though he was not there. "That was strange", he thought as he descended slowly. He circled the trees in a corkscrew fashion until he reached the ground, stumbling slightly as he landed. Biron walked up to his father, who did not look very excited at all.

"What are you doing, Biron?", he asked in disbelief. "Why are you playing such foolish games?"

Biron was stunned. Why was his father acting like this, he thought. He noticed that none of the other birds were standing near them. He assumed that it was because of himself and his flying.

"But dad, this isn't foolishness, it's flying." His father's face looked very serious, an intensity that Biron had never seen before.

"That is not flying, Biron. It's senseless and dangerous and I don't want to see you doing it again, do you hear me?"

"But why?" pleaded Biron.

"Because I am your father and I said so!"

Biron gave up, walking away broken hearted. He wanted to be by himself. He knew that his father was wrong and that flying was not foolish, but something that all birds were meant to do. He began to cry, not knowing why any of the other birds did not share his enthusiasm about flying. After all, it was the most exhilarating experience of his life.

"Maybe they did not want to be exhilarated. Maybe they felt comfortable with walking", he thought. Biron decided that he would only fly when his father was not present. His father had only said that he did not want to see him flying. Biron knew what his dad had meant, but there was nothing that was going to stop him from flying - not even the fear of disobeying his father.

84

Biron improved his flying skills steadily as the weeks went by. All of the other birds shunned him and his flying crusade. They were not about to admit that he was flying, or that any ideas they had were incorrect. A few birds secretly admired Biron and his flying, but did not want to admit it for fear of being rejected by the other birds. As he grew up, he left his parents' nest and built his own in a tree. He lived alone, separated from the other birds because of his flying, dropping in occasionally to see his parents. He tried to convert his mother to fly his way, but she was constantly telling him to come back to the ground.

"You will not get another bird to live with you in a nest built in the trees", she said. Biron always ended up arguing with her, as he wanted to do what he thought was correct. It made no sense to him to build his nest on the ground, as there was more protection in the trees and the views were spectacular. His mother wanted what she thought was best for him, believing that he would never find a mate that wanted to fly, and thought that he was wasting his life looking. Biron knew the type of bird that he was looking for. She would have to admire him for his flying and not be afraid of being rejected by the other birds - her parents included - when she learned to fly. Obviously she would need to fly if she was going to live in the trees. Biron wanted his chicks to learn to fly, and he knew that if their mother did not know how to, that they would be very confused indeed, especially with all of the other birds in the flock grounded. She would also have to be physically attractive to him - after all he was still an animal.

One morning while Biron was out practicing his flying, he spotted what seemed to be a bird in a distant tree. Without hesitation, he darted over to where she was perched.

"Hi, my name is Biron", he said. "And may I ask how you got into the trees like that?" "My name is Carmel and I flew up here", she retorted, slightly bemused by his question.

"Wow", said Biron, "Did you know that you are the first bird I have ever seen up here with me?" "No" she said, surprised. "I come from the large group of rocks over there", she pointed with her wing. "Most of us fly but a few have chosen to stay on the ground." "Really?" said Biron, "That's great. Can I pop over with you to see?" he pleaded. "Sure", Carmel replied, "let's go".

So Biron and Carmel flew over to the far valley, and thus began a new and fantastic phase of Biron's life.

The Beginning!

"Real art has the capacity to make us nervous"
Susan Sontag

About the Author

Des Sherlock is 52, an Industrial Designer, Entrepreneur, and amateur social analyist. He has spent over 26 years discovering and trying to live by the principles of Rethink Perfect in his personal and business life. He has spent a lot of this time consciously creating disputes and set about resolving them. He is not an academic and has no such qualifications in psychology or sociology. He is not an expert of any type and prefers to remain independent from such organisation with hierarchical structures unless they have an agreed set of rules of engagement such as Rethink Perfect uses.

He is a co-founder of an online startup, Oodles.com, with his brother Steve, and has also piloted a social venture called Quitober. He recently launched his latest venture, Tripcover.com.au a car rental excess insurance site.

He is proposing Rethink Perfect as a solution to moderate our own disputes. He is hoping to one day field test Rethink Perfect in a personal relationship.

Contact Des at des@rethinkperfect.com

"People ignore design that ignores people"
Frank Chimero

Contact Information:

Des Sherlock

Suite 243, 1B 192 Ann Street
Brisbane QLD Australia 4000

To offer any feedback:
http://twitter.com/rethinkperfect
http://RethinkPerfect.com
des@rethinkperfect.com

Bibliography

De Bono, Edward. **I Am Write You Are Wrong**. London: Viking, 1990

De Bono, Edward. **Think Before it's Too Late**. London: Vermilion, 2009

Robinson, Ken. **The Element**. NY: Penguin Group, 2009

Robinson, Ken. **Out of Our Minds**. W. Sussex: Capstone, 2001

Kawaski, Guy. **Enchantment**. NY: Penguin Group, 2011

Taleb, Nassim N. **Fooled by Randomness**. NY: Random House, 2004

Taleb, Nassim N. **Black Swan**. NY: Random House, 2010

Pirsig, Robert. **Zen & the Art**. New York: A Bantam Book, 1974

Maugham, W. Somerset. **The Razor's Edge**. NY: Doubleday, 1944

MacKay, Hugh. **What Makes us Tick**. Sydney: Hachette, 2000

Mauboussin, Hugh. **Think Twice**. Boston: Harvard Business, 2009

Orwell, Georg. **1984**. London: Penguin, 1950

Richard, Bach. **Jonathan Livingston Seagull**. NY: Avon Books, 1970

Mark, Joyner. **Simpleology**. New Jersey: J. Wiley & Son, 2007

Makridakis, Spyros – Hogarth, Robin – Anil Gaba. **Dance with Chance**. Oxford: Oneworld, 2009

www.ingramcontent.com/pod-product-compliance
Lightning Source LLC
Chambersburg PA
CBHW050546280326
41933CB00011B/1742